THE LEADER WAS ONCE A CHILD

DR. KARTIK NAGENDRAA
GAURI DAS

Clever Fox® PUBLISHING
Chennai • Bangalore

CLEVER FOX PUBLISHING
Chennai, India

Published by CLEVER FOX PUBLISHING 2026

ISBN: 978-93-7500-967-2

When we imagine what it is to be a leader, it's easy to ignore—or even bury—the past that shaped us. Yet, as The Leader Was Once a Child reveals, we do this at our peril. Our past matters. The more we acknowledge it, understand it, and honour the experiences that formed us, the deeper and more authentic our leadership becomes. This book invites every reader to look back with curiosity, because within those early stories lies the true foundation of who we are when we lead.

Lynda Gratton

Professor of Management Practice at London Business School &
Ranked by The Times as one of the top 15 Business Thinkers in the world

CONTENTS

FOREWORD

"The child is the father of the man" is a famous line written by the poet William Wordsworth, in one of his poems titled "My heart leaps up".

In this lovely book, the authors, Karthik Nagendra and Gauri Das, extend this poetic thought deep into our professional lives. They tell us how the child is not merely the father of the man, but is an abiding influence on the man's (or woman's) leadership.

This is a unique lens on leadership, because we often think of the impact that our bosses or company environments have had on our management styles, but rarely do we connect our leadership with our childhood.

Yet, as the authors highlight in this excellent treatise, so many of the positive qualities that leaders bring to the table, or indeed so many of the insecurities that we hold within ourselves, trace back to events of our childhood.

For instance, our tendency to either empower or to micromanage our teams may derive from what we witnessed or experienced when we were children. Similarly, many of our leadership beliefs may arise from our childhood stories – for instance, as the authors point out, an abiding distrust in senior management may have its roots in our father having lost his job unexpectedly because of some corporate restructuring in his company.

But why should we attempt to connect these dots between our leadership and our childhood? This book clearly sets out that the reason is not just to look back into our histories, but to chart out our futures in the most powerful, positive and constructive manner. When we understand the sources of our beliefs, we are in a far better position to identify our anchors and biases, to address the behaviours that hold us back, and to thereby unlock the true power that resides within us.

That is the true calling card of this book. It is about identifying, developing and using these insights about ourselves, many of which lie buried in our childhoods, to emerge stronger, and to transform how we think and act as leaders.

So many of us aspire be the best leaders that we can ever be. This book provides us a unique pathway to making this happen, through the stories it narrates, the insights it provokes and the framework it suggests. Happy reading !

Harish Bhat

Former Brand Custodian, Tata Sons.
Avid marketer and bestselling author.

INTRODUCTION

Rajiv sank into his office chair long after his team had left for the day. The board meeting had been rough— he'd snapped at a junior colleague over a minor error, and now guilt gnawed at him. "Why did I overreact like that?" he wondered. In the stillness of the empty office, a memory surfaced: a much younger Rajiv, trembling as his father scolded him harshly for a small mistake on a school assignment. That childhood scene, long buried, had quietly influenced his leadership style for years. Rajiv had always prided himself on being in control, yet under pressure his composure could crack in an all-too-familiar way. It struck him that the authoritative tone he had just used with his colleague was an echo of his father's voice. In that moment, Rajiv realized a profound truth: every leader's first lessons in leadership begin in childhood. Our earliest experiences—love and discipline, triumphs and traumas—plant the seeds of the behaviors and beliefs we carry into adulthood as leaders. We might outgrow our childhood shoes, but we never quite outgrow the influence of the child we once were.

We all intuitively know that childhood shapes the adults we become, but we often underestimate just how much our early years continue to affect how we lead . In fact, research suggests this influence may be even stronger for those in leadership roles . Leaders operate under intense pressures—rapid decision- making, large responsibilities, constant scrutiny—and in those high-pressure moments, we are most likely to revert to ingrained patterns formed long ago. A leader's default reactions to stress—whether it's to remain calm or to panic, to listen or to dominate, to trust or to micromanage—often trace back to coping strategies learned in childhood. As leadership consultant Nik Kinley observes, when time for deliberate thought shrinks, "it's in moments like these that we are most susceptible to the influence of the past" . The child within quietly but powerfully informs the leader we are today.

Consider some real examples. Harjeet, a senior finance leader, recalls enduring frequent long power outages as a child in his small hometown. The boredom and frustration he felt were tempered by watching his parents remain patient and optimistic in the darkness. Decades later, Harjeet's colleagues admire his uncanny calm during workplace crises—the servers go down or a project derails, yet he navigates the challenge with steady resilience. It's no accident: the patience learned in those candle-lit childhood nights became a cornerstone of his leadership style . Harjeet can trace other traits back to youth as well. His action-oriented approach to problem-solving, for instance, was modeled by his mother. He fondly recounts how she once rallied neighbors to clear a dangerous makeshift market blocking their street, demonstrating *leadership through action* rather than words. That memory instilled in him a bias for proactive leadership—seeing a problem and tackling it head-on .

Another leader, Sangeeta Raised in a joint family, learned early how to navigate conflict, read people, and adapt communication styles. A childhood incident where boys claimed girls couldn't excel in math ignited her competitive drive. As a leader, she champions adaptability and as a leadership coach, she empowers others to challenge limiting beliefs.

Giovanni's story mirrors this pattern from a very different geography. Growing up in a small Sicilian town, he absorbed an early lesson from his father, a modest construction entrepreneur: nothing is given, everything is earned. When Giovanni lost his father at twelve, that belief hardened into resolve, reinforced by a mother who insisted he continue his education despite financial strain. Moving from Sicily to Milan, then London and Malta, exposure to different cultures gradually softened any rigid worldview, teaching him that integrity and goodness are not bound by nationality or religion. Today, as a Chief Risk Officer, Giovanni leads with quiet humility rather than hierarchy. He sits alongside his team, takes notes in meetings, invites ideas from every level, and believes the best idea should lead, not the loudest title. Failure, to him, is instruction, not stigma. His ambition is to make himself unnecessary by building others up. The resilience of loss, the discipline of scarcity, and the openness shaped by travel together define a leadership style grounded in trust, empathy, and shared ownership.

Nomadic childhood experiences shape you in powerful ways — they teach adaptability, curiosity, and the ability to connect quickly. Harish Bhat grew up moving across cities in Tamil Nadu and Kerala because his father, a public sector bank officer, was transferred every few years. From the grandeur of Madurai's temple to the quiet backwaters of Kollam, each place left an imprint on his imagination. Never a long-settled insider, he learned to build relationships intentionally, adjusting to new schools and cultures with ease. Alongside these moves, he discovered a love for writing, spending hours on his manual Godrej typewriter and even winning an international writing prize at fourteen. These early experiences — constant relocation, close observation, and creative expression — shaped his leadership style. They made him resilient, open to change, clear in communication, and comfortable connecting with people anywhere — qualities that later defined his success as a corporate leader.

Even aspects of family structure and upbringing leave an imprint. Michelle, an HR leader and leadership coach, notes that being a middle child shaped her leadership in subtle ways . Sandwiched between an overachieving older brother and a mischievous younger sister, she often played the *peacemaker* and learned to lead through influence rather than authority. Michelle also points out that the overall *family climate*—whether supportive or challenging—deeply impacts a child's confidence and willingness to take risks . A nurturing environment can instill a secure base of self-belief, whereas a critical or unpredictable one can make a future leader more cautious or prone to self-doubt. In Michelle's case, her parents' constant encouragement in sports and school gave her the confidence to step up and take initiative in team settings.

Later, as a leader, she noticed that colleagues who grew up in more critical households were often more anxious about failure and less likely to speak up with bold ideas. These patterns were not fixed destinies, but they were powerful starting points for each person's leadership journey.

Throughout this book, we will explore in depth how childhood experiences cast long shadows—and shining lights—on our adult leadership style. We'll delve into psychological theories that help explain this phenomenon, from attachment theory (how our early bonds shape the way we build trust and relationships) to emotional intelligence (how we learn—or don't learn—to understand and manage emotions early on) to schema therapy (how core beliefs formed in childhood can become "life scripts" that leaders either remain trapped in or learn to rewrite). We will hear the stories of real leaders (disguised where needed for privacy) from diverse industries and cultures, each illustrating a facet of the central theme: before you were a leader, you were a child, and that child within still influences the leader you have become.

Most importantly, this is a book of practical transformation. It is not about blaming our parents or the past; it's about gaining *self-awareness* and then taking *action* to become a better leader. Each chapter will provide tools, frameworks, and exercises to connect the dots between childhood and leadership, and to actively shape a more conscious, effective leadership style going forward. You will find checklists for reflection, self-assessments, and prompts to help you excavate your own formative experiences. You will discover frameworks like the Attachment Styles in Leadership model that links early bonding with leadership behaviors, an

Emotional Intelligence development chart that maps personal growth, a Leadership Blind Spots Matrix to identify what you might be missing about yourself, a Personal Leadership Narrative Rewrite template to help you reframe limiting beliefs, a Trust-Building Toolkit for strengthening relationships with your team, and a Trigger Response Plan to manage emotional reactions. These are not abstract theories, but *practical playbooks* you can use in your daily leadership life.

The book is organized into three parts to mirror a journey of self-discovery and growth:

- Part I: Foundations – We lay the groundwork by examining how key psychological foundations formed in childhood (attachment, emotional development, early belief systems) manifest in adult leadership. Understanding these connections is the first step toward growth.
- Part II: Excavation – We then turn inward, with guided introspection to "excavate" your own childhood influences. We provide tools to uncover hidden blind spots, identify emotional triggers, and recognize patterns that originated in your early years. This middle section is reflective and at times revelatory—you may unearth long-forgotten memories that explain current behaviors.
- Part III: Transformation – Finally, we focus on change and growth. With self-awareness in hand, we introduce strategies to *transform* your leadership style. You'll learn how to rewrite negative narratives into positive ones, develop greater emotional intelligence and resilience, build trust and psychological safety in your team, and integrate your newfound insights into your everyday leadership practice. This part is about taking action to become the leader you aspire to be, while honoring the lessons of the child you once were.

Throughout the journey, we maintain a story-driven, human-centric approach. Each chapter opens with real-life stories and scenarios that draw you in and reflect on your own experience. The tone is conversational and candid—we are fellow travelers on this path, not distant academics pontificating. You'll find moments of personal reflection from leaders who have walked this road of linking past to present. Many have found that acknowledging their inner child made them *more* effective, not less—more empathetic, more creative, and more resilient. By the end of the book, I hope you will share that conclusion and feel empowered with clarity, tools, and motivation to continue growing.

Before we dive in, keep one guiding thought in mind: the child you were is not a shackle, but a source of insight and strength. As the saying goes, "The child is father of the man" – our younger selves have much to teach us, if we are willing to listen. By courageously revisiting our early chapters, we can write more authentic and impactful later chapters in our leadership story. So let's begin this journey of reflection and transformation. After all, every leader was once a child – and within every leader, that child is still very much alive, waiting to be understood.

PART I

FOUNDATIONS – EARLY EXPERIENCES THAT SHAPE LEADERS

Even the tallest tree draws its strength from its roots. In Part I, we examine the root system of leadership – the foundational experiences and psychological patterns from childhood that underlie adult leadership behavior. We explore how our earliest relationships teach us to trust (or not), how we learn to understand emotions by watching caregivers, and how the beliefs we internalize as children can become the invisible scripts running in the background of our leadership decisions. These four chapters build the groundwork of knowledge and insight, preparing us to dig deeper into our personal stories in Part II.

CHAPTER 1

THE PAST IN THE PRESENT – HOW CHILDHOOD SHAPES LEADERSHIP

On the surface, Ajay was every bit the confident startup CEO—decisive, bold, and seemingly unflappable. But when his company's big product launch faltered and investors started pressuring him, his façade cracked. He grew defensive in meetings and avoided difficult conversations. Puzzled by his own behavior, Ajay sought coaching. In one session, a simple question caught him off guard: "When is the first time you remember feeling like this?" Memories flooded back: as a child, Ajay had often felt cornered by an overbearing uncle who would criticize him harshly whenever he made a mistake. As an adult, the investor pressure was unconsciously triggering those old feelings of being a scolded ten-year-old, and Ajay's instinctive response was still to shrink or become defensive. This realization was a turning point. *The child he had been was influencing the leader he was now.* With this awareness, Ajay could begin to change his reactions. His story is not unique; in fact, it's remarkably common. If you look closely at any leader's moments of greatest strain or stress, you will often find the imprint of childhood experiences guiding their responses.

In this opening chapter, we explore the general principle that our leadership approach today is a product of experiences and lessons—positive and negative—from our early years. It's an intuitive idea backed by growing research. For example, psychologists Shlomo Ben-Hur and Nik Kinley note that leaders tend to "present an image of being in control," but under pressure, when there's no time to carefully manage that image, old patterns assert themselves . They identified *optimism versus pessimism* and *composure versus reactivity* as two critical tendencies in leaders that often trace back to childhood influences. We'll delve into those specific traits in the next chapters; here, let's establish the broad landscape of how childhood can shape leadership identity.

Early Role Models and Scripts: One of the most straightforward ways childhood shapes us is through the role models we observe. Children are keen observers; they watch how parents, older siblings, or community leaders handle situations and often internalize those approaches. *Leadership is first learned by imitation.* If you grew up with a parent who led with compassion and patience, you likely absorbed that style. If your primary example of authority was domineering or volatile, you might either emulate that or react against it in your own leadership. Harjeet's story from the Introduction is a vivid example: seeing his mother identify a neighborhood problem and rally others to fix it taught him that a leader is someone who takes initiative and serves their community . As a result, Harjeet's default setting as a leader is to roll up his sleeves and solve problems alongside his team. He leads by example, just as his mother did.

On the other hand, consider a case where the early model was negative. Ravi, a successful corporate strategist, grew up under a demanding coach who believed in tough love. The experience shaped his discipline and high standards. But this was not Ravi's natural style so he retained his focus on excellence while leading with greater empathy and encouragement.

Ravi often felt he was "never good enough" in that coach's eyes. In his early years as a manager, he unconsciously replicated this script with his subordinates: he was extremely demanding and sparing with praise, thinking it would spur excellence. Instead, it demoralized his team. Only after a frank 360-degree feedback (and some soul-searching) did Ravi realize he had become the very figure he resented in youth. He had to consciously *unlearn* that model (we'll revisit how he did so in Part III). This illustrates how early role models can cast long shadows—we might inhabit their style without realizing it, until evidence or reflection brings it to light.

As we spoke with another leader, Sujeet, now the CEO of a global organization, he quickly traced his leadership instincts back to his early years. Strong family values and formative years in the National Cadet Corps (NCC) instilled in Sujeet discipline, courage, and emotional steadiness. Early experiences in community leadership and sport taught him that true strength lies in overcoming self-doubt and supporting others. As a leader, he recognised how fear silently limits potential and built cultures centred on mentoring and psychological safety—where people perform with confidence and accountability.

Core Values and Assumptions: Many leaders find that their deepest values and assumptions about people and work have roots in childhood. For example, trust (or mistrust) is often a value shaped early. A leader who grew up in an environment where trust was abundant—say, a family that communicated openly and kept promises—may have an easier time extending trust to colleagues and expecting goodwill. In contrast, a leader whose childhood was marked by broken promises or instability may instinctively be more guarded, even cynical, believing "it's safer not to trust anyone completely." These early-formed assumptions can significantly influence one's leadership: whether you delegate or micromanage, whether you build collaborative teams or prefer strict control, can hinge on how safe or threatened you feel trusting others. We'll explore the link between childhood attachment and adult trust in Chapter 2, but suffice it to say the basic stance of "people are generally trustworthy" versus "people will let you down" is often set in the formative years.

Another example is the value of achievement. Some leaders internalize a message from childhood that their worth comes from achievement and hard work—perhaps because they received praise chiefly when they excelled in school or sports. This can drive a tremendous work ethic and success, but it can also lead to perfectionism and difficulty relaxing. Psychologists call such deeply ingrained patterns "schemas." A schema is essentially a belief or feeling about oneself and the world that forms early and then perpetuates into adulthood, often unconsciously . A child who learns "I must be perfect to be loved" may become a leader with an *unrelenting standards* schema, pushing themselves and their team mercilessly. In one study of executives, nearly 50% showed significant signs of an *Unrelenting Standards* schema, making it the most common early schema among that leadership sample . We will dive deeper into schemas and beliefs in Chapter 4, but the key point here is: the stories we start telling ourselves as children—about our worth, about how the world works—often become the scripts we carry into our leadership roles. Recognizing these scripts is the first step to changing the ones that no longer serve us.

Building on this insight, Sujeet also spoke about how childhood influences do not stop with the leader alone—they quietly shape the people they lead as well. Over time, he began to notice familiar patterns within his teams: hesitation in decision-making, an excessive fear of failure, or a tendency to play it safe. Often, these behaviors echoed early conditioning rather than present-day capability. By observing patiently, mentoring deliberately, and fostering psychological safety, Sujeet learned to help individuals move past these invisible limits. In his view, while formative experiences leave a deep imprint, it is awareness and intentional growth that enable leaders to unlock potential and cultivate stronger, more confident teams.

Personality and Temperament: Not everything is nurture—nature plays a role too. Children are born with different temperaments: some are naturally more anxious, others more bold. These inborn tendencies interact with our environment. A naturally timid child might become more confident if raised in a supportive environment, or more anxious if raised in a critical one. By adulthood, we have a unique personality shaped by that interplay. Certain personality traits clearly affect leadership style: extroversion vs. introversion, for instance, or being more analytical vs. more empathetic. While temperament is partly genetic, childhood is when it's either reinforced or reshaped. If you were the shy kid who was gently encouraged to take on leadership in small ways (maybe you were asked to be class monitor, or lead a scout project), you might have developed social confidence despite initial introversion. Conversely, a naturally outgoing child who faced constant rejection or ridicule might grow more cautious socially. As leaders, understanding that some of our tendencies are long-standing parts of who we are (and not flaws) can be freeing. It allows us to leverage strengths and manage weaknesses without self-judgment. For example, a leader who knows they've always been introverted can accept that they excel in thoughtful analysis and one-on-one influence, while perhaps needing to push themselves in big networking events or public speaking. The past provides context that can engender *self-compassion*—"I've always been this way, and that's okay; now how do I work with it?"—instead of frustration.

Cultural and Societal Influences: Childhood influence is not only about family; it's also about the broader culture and society in which we grow up. Norms around authority, communication, and gender roles vary widely and inform how we later lead. For instance, someone raised in a culture that values deference to elders and quiet obedience may, as a leader, find it uncomfortable to engage in direct confrontation or open dissent in meetings. They might need to learn that in some business contexts, debate and even disagreement with higher-ups is not disrespectful but healthy. On the flip side, someone from a very individualistic culture might need to learn to dial back and listen more when leading a multicultural team. Gender socialization in childhood also plays a role. Sangeetha's recollection of being told "girls can't do X" lit a fire in her to prove otherwise . Many women leaders carry early experiences of gender bias that both motivate them and also sometimes burden them (e.g. feeling they must be "twice as good" to succeed). Male leaders, who as boys may have been taught to "toughen up" and not show vulnerability, might struggle later with emotional openness or empathy—key leadership skills in today's world. Throughout this book, we will be attentive to how these cultural childhood influences appear in leadership, and how to become aware of and adapt them when needed.

A Continuum, Not a Cage: It's crucial to emphasize that childhood influences are significant but not deterministic. Humans are remarkably capable of change. An anxious child can become a bold leader; a headstrong child can learn humility. Early influences create a *starting point,* a kind of default setting, but they do not lock us in. As one expert put it, early experiences "inform who we are and who we can be" rather than chaining us. We carry our past into the present, but with self-awareness and effort, we can choose which parts of that past to nurture and which to transform . The coming chapters will give many examples of leaders who did exactly that: they identified a trait or belief formed in childhood that was limiting their effectiveness, and they actively worked to change it – thereby effectively re-parenting their inner child in a more empowering way.

For now, reflect on your own general stance as a leader. What's your instinct under pressure? To control, to appease, to avoid, to confront?

Where might that instinct come from in your early life? Begin noticing these connections in day-to-day moments. When you feel particularly *childlike* in your reactions – maybe unusually insecure when receiving criticism (like Ajay did), or fiercely competitive when someone challenges you (like Sangeetha in school) – pause and ask, "What does this remind me of from when I was younger?" You might be surprised by the memories or feelings that surface. This book will help you make sense of those connections.

In the chapters ahead, we move from this general premise to specific foundational lenses: attachment, emotion, and belief. Each topic will deepen our understanding of the past-present link in leadership. Keep Ajay's story, Harjeet's patience, Sangeetha's adaptability, and your own emerging insights in mind as we proceed. Leadership is often described as a journey; it may be more accurate to say it's a *continuation* of a journey that began in childhood. By looking back at where we started, we can better navigate where we go next.

CHAPTER 2

TRUST BEGINS AT HOME – ATTACHMENT STYLES IN LEADERSHIP

At a team offsite, Lena, a department head, facilitated a trust-building exercise. She noticed an interesting pattern: some managers readily shared personal stories and vulnerabilities with their colleagues, quickly forging a sense of camaraderie. Others participated warily, revealing little and even making light of the activity. Later that evening, in an informal chat by the campfire, the conversation turned to childhoods. Lena was struck by how the managers who were most open tended to describe warm, supportive upbringings— one spoke of parents who were "always there to listen." In contrast, those who were reserved mentioned things like "My dad was a military man, very strict" or "I learned early to be self-reliant; my folks weren't the touchy-feely type." This wasn't a rigorous scientific study, but Lena had stumbled onto a powerful insight: the way we learned to relate to our caregivers as children profoundly influences how we relate to people as leaders. In psychological terms, childhood forms our *attachment style*, which becomes the blueprint for trust, communication, and connection in our adult relationships —including the workplace.

Attachment theory originated in the work of John Bowlby and Mary Ainsworth, who studied how infants bond with caregivers. They identified patterns like secure, anxious, and avoidant attachment. These patterns aren't just about infants—they tend to carry forward into adulthood, affecting how we behave in friendships, romances, and yes, professional teams . When you become a leader, your attachment style doesn't vanish at the office door. It subtly shapes whether you *trust your team*, how you handle conflict, and how you motivate and support others. Do you feel comfortable delegating (trusting others to do things well)? Do you crave lots of feedback and reassurance? Do you shy away from giving tough feedback to avoid conflict? The answers often lie in attachment-driven instincts.

To understand this better, let's briefly outline the main adult attachment styles and how they might manifest in leadership:

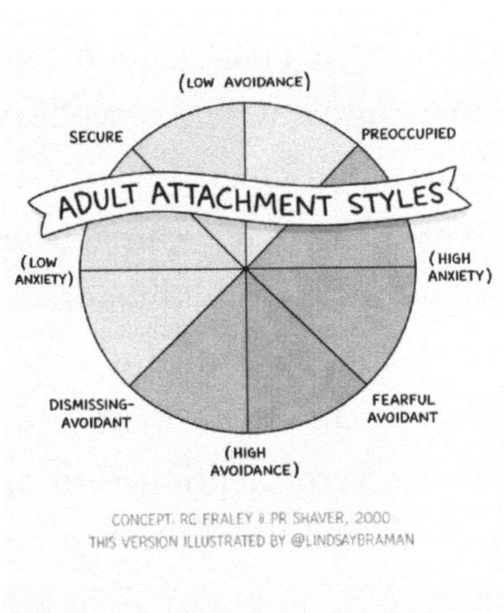

Adapted figure: The four adult attachment styles, often depicted in a two-axis diagram of anxiety and avoidance. "Secure" (low avoidance, low anxiety) sits at the ideal balance; "Anxious" (low avoidance, high anxiety) craves connection but fears rejection; "Avoidant" (high avoidance, low anxiety) values independence over closeness; "Fearful-Disorganized" (high avoidance, high anxiety) experiences internal conflict in relationships. Leaders often subconsciously lead from one of these styles until they build self-awareness to grow more secure.

- Secure Attachment – *Comfortable with closeness and autonomy.* A leader with a secure style tends to trust others and be trusted in return. They strike a balance between guiding the team and giving space. Secure leaders are often confident, empathetic, and not threatened by others' competence. They build strong relationships at work because their default assumption is positive: they assume people generally mean well and that together they can handle challenges. Strengths of secure leaders include being good listeners and mentors, and maintaining a calm, solution-focused approach in conflict. If anything, a potential pitfall is that secure leaders may sometimes prioritize harmony too much—occasionally avoiding tough feedback or conflict in an effort to keep relationships smooth. However, overall this style is a sweet spot most leaders would benefit from cultivating, as we'll discuss later in this chapter.

Anxious (Preoccupied) Attachment – *Craves connection and approval, but fears rejection or inadequacy.* An anxiously attached leader is deeply invested in relationships and team morale— perhaps too invested. On the positive side, these leaders are often highly attuned to their team's needs and emotions . They care a great deal about making their people feel supported. However, their insecurity can lead to micromanaging ("I just want to make sure everything is okay") or seeking constant validation ("Is the team happy with my decision? Do they like me as a boss?") . They might struggle to give autonomy, worrying that if a team member struggles, it reflects on them. Decision-making can also suffer, as anxious leaders may second-guess themselves or overthink every choice in an attempt to avoid anyone's disapproval . For example, Sangeetha recalled a client—an extremely technically skilled manager—who felt insecure about his communication because he hadn't gone to an English-medium school. His anxious self-doubt led him to overprepare for every presentation and overly defer to others in meetings. With coaching, he highlighted his strengths and achievements, which helped him break the limiting belief and grow more confident . As he became more secure, he could lead without constantly fearing he wasn't good enough. Anxious-style leaders benefit from learning to self-soothe their fear of failure and from trusting their team (and themselves) more.

Avoidant (Dismissive) Attachment – *Values independence and self-reliance, often uncomfortable with too much closeness.* A leader with an avoidant style typically trusts their own abilities more than others' and may keep an emotional distance from their team . Such leaders are often very competent and analytical – they excel in strategic thinking or technical skills, which they may have dived into as a safe zone instead of dealing with messy human emotions . They often give team members a lot of autonomy (which can be positive), but might provide little emotional support or feedback. Team members could experience them as *distant, unapproachable,* or overly critical without the soft edges. Avoidant leaders also tend to shy away from showing vulnerability; they may not admit when they're overwhelmed or ask for help, because their core belief is "I can't rely on others." The risk here is a lack of team cohesion or trust – employees might feel their avoidant boss doesn't care about them, or they never truly know what the boss is thinking. For instance, Vasuta Agarwal, a senior business leader raised to be self-sufficient in a unique combination of an academic and business family household, Vasuta led with extreme independence and emotional resilience. Over time, she realised her inability to be vulnerable was limiting team trust. She consciously learned to combine autonomy with openness and warmth.

Disorganized (Fearful) Attachment – *Marked by internal conflict: a desire for connection but a deep fear of trust.* Leaders with a disorganized style can be inconsistent – charming and supportive one day, withdrawn or explosive the next . This often stems from chaotic or traumatic early experiences, where the very people one turns to for safety were sources of fear or unpredictability. In leadership, this style is fortunately less common at high levels (severe attachment wounds can impede career progression unless addressed), but it does appear. Such a leader might send mixed signals: for example, encouraging the team to come to them with problems, but then reacting with anger when someone admits a mistake, leaving everyone confused and cautious. Or they may form close bonds with team members then suddenly pull back or sabotage those relationships due to mistrust. The *strengths* sometimes observed in disorganized leaders include creativity and crisis performance – because they have lived with turmoil, they might excel in high-pressure scenarios, pulling off ingenious solutions in a pinch . However, the *risks* are significant: their inconsistency can breed confusion and anxiety in teams . Employees may feel like they're "walking on eggshells," never sure which version of the boss they'll get. A real-life example: a startup CTO, brilliant in technical vision (moments of brilliance under pressure, as noted) , had a habit of alternating between praising and harshly vilifying the same team members. His team's morale plummeted, and turnover was high, even though they respected his intellect. With coaching (and therapy), he realized these patterns mirrored his own childhood with an abusive parent. He began intensive work to develop a secure base in himself and to communicate more consistently. Over time, he greatly improved, but it required confronting deep fears and working on emotional regulation (something we'll cover in Chapter 10 on emotional mastery).

These styles are not binary labels; think of them as points on a spectrum or tendencies that can mix. Also, crucially, attachment styles can evolve. No one is permanently stuck as "avoidant" or "anxious." With intention and new experiences, people can move toward secure attachment. In fact, psychology research talks about "earned secure attachment" – when someone with an insecure style consciously learns and adopts more secure ways of relating, often through healing relationships or coaching . This is empowering: your childhood set the initial coordinates, but you can absolutely chart a new course. Leadership development, at its heart, often involves moving towards the behaviors of a securely attached leader: greater self-awareness, balanced concern for tasks and people, openness to feedback, and comfort with both autonomy and collaboration.

Attachment at Work: What does all this theory mean for you as a leader day-to-day? It means your interactions with your team are likely influenced by these ingrained patterns of trust and relationship. For instance:

- If you tend to micromanage and find it hard to delegate, ask yourself if this relates to an anxious worry that "things will go wrong if I'm not overseeing everything" or perhaps a deep need to prove yourself (seeking approval). Recognizing the anxious attachment tendency can prompt you to practice letting go in small steps, building confidence that others can handle tasks. A checklist for anxious leaders might be: *Have I clearly defined the outcome and then given my team member space to execute?* If the urge to hover arises, recall that this might be an old fear talking, not present reality.
- If you avoid difficult conversations or check out emotionally when conflict arises, this might echo an avoidant style. An avoidant leader might rationalize, "It's not worth the drama, I'll just send an email," but the team senses the distance. The growth step here is to push slightly past your comfort zone in connecting with your team. Try *one* personal check-in where you'd normally skip it ("How was your weekend?" or "I noticed you seemed frustrated in the meeting—anything you want to discuss?"). It may feel unnatural at first, but small consistent efforts can soften an avoidant edge and build trust. Also, remind yourself that giving feedback or addressing conflict, though uncomfortable, is an act of respect for your team—they generally would prefer to hear from you than guess at your silence.
- If you see inconsistency in your leadership—like sometimes you're very supportive, other times you're irritated and impatient without clear reason—it's worth reflecting if some trigger is activating a

disorganized pattern. Do you have an employee who somehow reminds you (emotionally) of someone from your past? Are you reacting to them and not entirely sure why? This might be a transfer of a past relationship dynamic. Becoming aware is key; you might even enlist a coach or mentor to observe and give feedback on consistent versus inconsistent behaviors. Mindfulness practices (discussed later) can also help you stay centered so you respond to the person in front of you, not the ghost of someone behind you.

One useful tool to start applying attachment theory to your leadership is to identify your own attachment style tendencies. Here are a few reflection prompts (adapted from psychology research):

- Think about how you respond when a high-stakes project goes awry or when you receive tough feedback. Do you seek support and advice from colleagues (leaning on relationships), or do you withdraw to handle it solo? Do you become overly anxious about others' opinions of you in that moment? Notice these reactions.
- Consider feedback you've received about your management style. Has anyone said you "micromanage" or conversely that you're "difficult to read" or "not available enough"? Such themes can hint at underlying attachment-driven behavior (micromanage might hint at anxious control; being distant at avoidant tendencies).
- Reflect on your comfort with trust: Do you generally trust your team members easily until proven otherwise (a more secure stance), or do you feel you must "verify" everything and that trust must be earned slowly? How about *your* approach to trusting your bosses or peers? Patterns upwards can mirror patterns downwards.
- You might also consider taking a formal attachment style questionnaire, or working with a coach or therapist trained in these concepts, to get a clearer picture. The goal is not to pigeonhole yourself, but to increase self-awareness.

Let's bring this to life with a composite story: Daniel, a middle manager, always prided himself on being self-sufficient. He rarely asked his boss for help and found one-on-one check-ins with his own team members somewhat uncomfortable. When a promotion put him in charge of a larger team, cracks appeared. He was seen as aloof and unapproachable; minor issues in the team blew up because people didn't feel they could come to Daniel early on. In coaching, Daniel traced this pattern back to childhood: he had grown up essentially raising himself, as his parents worked long hours. He learned "don't depend on anyone" and carried that avoidant attachment ethos into leadership. Realizing this, Daniel decided to consciously experiment with new behaviors: he started having brief daily huddles to signal openness, and he made it a point to praise team members' good work regularly (something he'd never done). Over a few months, his team's trust in him grew, and he was pleasantly surprised to find that leaning into relationships did not weaken performance—it enhanced it. By becoming a bit more "secure" in attachment behavior, Daniel unlocked greater loyalty and productivity in his team.

The takeaway for leaders is powerful: if you understand your attachment style, you gain a lever for improving your leadership relationships. A leader who becomes more secure (whether they start anxious or avoidant) will generally see positive ripple effects: communication improves, team members feel safer (we'll talk about psychological safety in Chapter 11), and performance often follows. In fact, a study in *Psychology Today* notes that secure leaders often excel at balancing results with relationships—they maintain clear vision and trust within teams . They're empathetic but also confident decision-makers. The good news is that even if you didn't have a "secure" start in life, you can cultivate secure behaviors now.

Developing a More Secure Leadership Style: Here are some actionable strategies for moving toward secure attachment in your leadership (many of these are useful for anyone, regardless of starting style):

- *Build Self-Awareness (Know Your Triggers):* Pay attention to when you feel stressed in relationships at work. What triggers you? Is it when someone challenges you (making you want to either appease them or dismiss them)? When you feel someone is checking on your work (does that spark defensiveness)? By identifying triggers, you can separate *current situations* from *old attachment fears.* We'll cover triggers more in Chapter 7, but start noting them now. For example, Lena (from the offsite story) realized she got unusually anxious when her manager was very hands-on with her work —it traced to feeling scrutinized by a parent. Recognizing this, she could remind herself that her current manager's behavior was about the work, not a lack of trust in her as a person, and she responded more calmly.

Practice Empathy and Active Listening: Secure attachment correlates with higher empathy – the ability to step into others' shoes. You can boost this by intentionally listening more in conversations, asking questions, and summarizing what you heard to ensure understanding. Not only does this help you understand your team's needs, it also signals to them that you value and respect them, thereby building trust. Harjeet's transformation from an overly talkative leader to an active listener is a perfect case: he observed that great leaders listen more than they speak, so he trained himself to hold back and truly hear others . This shift dramatically improved his team's trust in him and their performance. Listening is essentially an attachment-building activity—it strengthens your bond with the team.

Invite and Embrace Feedback: As Michelle advised to the leaders she coaches, *seeking feedback regularly* is crucial . Secure leaders aren't afraid of feedback; they see it as growth fuel. By actively asking your team, peers, and superiors how you're doing and what you can improve, you demonstrate confidence and openness. This can be tough if you have an anxious style (you might fear negative feedback greatly) or if avoidant (you might feel it's pointless or threatening). But consider feedback as an investment in security: the more you know, the less you have to assume or fear. Also, by receiving feedback non-defensively, you show your team it's safe to be honest – a hallmark of a secure, trusting environment.

- *Mindfulness and Emotional Regulation:* Practicing mindfulness or any form of self-reflection (journaling, meditation, prayer – whatever suits you) can help you stay grounded in the present rather than getting hijacked by past anxieties. Mindfulness is proven to help individuals respond rather than react. If you're anxiously inclined, it helps you observe your anxious thoughts without immediately obeying them. If you're avoidant, it helps you notice emotions you might normally push away. Even a simple habit like a few deep breaths before responding to an emotionally charged situation can invoke the calm, wise leader in you rather than the frightened child. We'll expand on techniques in Chapter 10, but it's worth starting with small practices early on.
- *Set Healthy Boundaries:* This might sound counter-intuitive in a chapter about trust and attachment, but secure relationships actually have clear boundaries. If you are anxiously attached, you may need to learn not to overstep in seeking reassurance, and if avoidant, you may need to open up more—but in both cases, being clear about expectations and limits improves security

For a leader, this means communicate your availability ("I'm here for you, but I also trust you to run with this. Let's check in next week."), establish norms (like "We can disagree in meetings, but we do so respectfully."), and respect your team members' boundaries too. Boundaries create a sense of safety because everyone knows where they stand.

Consider Professional Guidance: If you identify strongly with having insecure attachment tendencies that significantly impact your leadership (e.g., crippling fear of criticism, or inability to connect with anyone at work), it can be very helpful to work with a therapist or coach on these specific issues . It's not weak to seek help; on the contrary, it shows commitment to growth. Some leaders in our stories did just that—Ravi, for instance, admitted he never thought about childhood influences until a coach prompted him . That reflection opened new doors for him in how he led (we'll hear more about him later). Sometimes an outside perspective accelerates the process of "re- attaching" more securely by providing a new model of trust in the therapeutic or coaching relationship.

In closing this chapter, remember Lena's observation at the offsite: those who *could* trust and share were not inherently "better" managers—they simply had a head start from past experiences that made trust their default. Those who hung back weren't "bad" either; they had protective walls built long ago for good reasons. The wonderful thing about adulthood is we can renovate those walls—take some down, reinforce others with healthier material. Leadership is relational. By understanding the template your childhood gave you for relationships, you gain the power to reshape it. When leaders work on their attachment style, the effects ripple outward: teams become more engaged and loyal, conflicts are navigated more openly, and a culture of trust begins to flourish.

So ask yourself: *How was trust modeled to me as a child? Do I push people away or hold them too close? What kind of secure behaviors can I practice this week?* Maybe it's as simple as telling a trusted colleague, "I realized I sometimes hesitate to delegate because I worry about things going wrong. I'm working on trusting the team more. Can you give me a nudge if you see me micromanaging?" Such honesty itself is a secure act. It might feel vulnerable, but it builds real connection.

In the next chapter, we'll continue laying foundations by looking at another childhood influence: how we learn (or don't learn) to understand and manage emotions. Emotional intelligence in leadership has been hailed as a make-or-break skill. As we'll see, the seeds of emotional intelligence are planted early in life. Whether they were nurtured or neglected can make a noticeable difference in one's leadership style – but like attachment, emotional skills can be developed at any stage. With an understanding of our attachment style in hand, we now turn to the emotional climate of childhood and its impact on the leader's self-control and empathy.

CHAPTER 3

EARLY EMOTIONAL LESSONS – THE ROOTS OF EMOTIONAL INTELLIGENCE

One evening, Keiko, a project manager known for her steady demeanor, found herself in an argument with a peer from another department. Voices were raised. Later, as she cooled down, Keiko was mortified — it was the first time she'd *lost her temper* at work. "That's not me," she thought. When asked by her boss what had triggered her outburst, tears welled up in Keiko's eyes. She realized the confrontation had made her feel *helpless*, a feeling she despised. Digging deeper, she recalled childhood moments of being bullied in school, how she had come home crying until her father told her sternly to "stop being a baby and toughen up." From that day, she vowed never to show tears or anger, bottling up her emotions. But bottled emotions have a way of exploding under pressure. The workplace argument uncorked years of suppressed frustration. Keiko's story illustrates a crucial point: our ability to understand and manage emotions – in ourselves and others – is shaped by how we learned to deal with feelings early in life. Emotional intelligence (EI) is often talked about as a key leadership skill; here we see its foundation is laid in childhood.

Daniel Goleman, who popularized Emotional Intelligence, describes it as a set of competencies grouped in areas like self-awareness, self-regulation, empathy (social awareness), and social skill (relationship management). These competencies don't magically appear when you become a manager; they develop (or don't) throughout one's upbringing and formative years. Were you encouraged to name and talk about feelings, or told to "suck it up"? Did you see adults handle conflicts calmly, or erupt in anger? Did your family model empathy and listening, or was it a "children should be seen, not heard" environment? Such experiences quietly teach you *emotional habits*. The good news is, like attachment styles, emotional habits can be re-learned and improved. But first, you have to recognize what you were implicitly taught about emotions as a child, because those lessons may be affecting your leadership style more than you know. Let's break down two major facets of emotional intelligence in leadership that have clear roots in childhood: optimism vs. pessimism (which relates to one's outlook and resilience) and emotion regulation vs. expression (how one handles strong feelings).

Optimism vs. Pessimism – The Outlook Instilled Early: Imagine two executives, Asha and Ben, facing an identical setback: their product launch fails to meet targets. Asha reacts by saying, "This is a temporary setback. We learned some valuable lessons, and we'll find a new opportunity." Ben reacts with, "This is a disaster. I knew things were too good to last; what if everything falls apart now?" These differing explanatory styles – optimistic vs. pessimistic – can greatly influence how they lead their teams through the challenge. Research indicates that whether a person leans optimistic or pessimistic is partly genetic but significantly shaped by childhood experiences Three particular childhood factors stand out :

- Parental Positivity: Children often adopt a similar level of optimism or pessimism as their parents If you grew up with caregivers who generally expected good outcomes and looked on the bright side, you likely absorbed that positivity. Conversely, if the tone at home was "Life is hard and things usually go wrong," you may carry a cautious or negative outlook. This doesn't mean you're doomed to it; awareness is key. (Ask yourself: do you hear one of your parent's voices when you appraise a situation? Many of us do.)

Affection and Emotional Support: Studies show that when parents are affectionate and sensitive to a child's emotional needs, that child tends to develop a more optimistic attitude. Warmth breeds a fundamental sense that the world is safe and that things will be okay. On the other hand, a lack of warmth or emotional neglect correlates with a more pessimistic, mistrustful outlook . For example, a leader who as a child rarely received comfort might, as an adult, struggle to believe that events will turn out fine – they never had someone helping them regulate fear or sadness, so those feelings loom larger.

Parental Strictness/Authoritarianism: Interestingly, research cited by Kinley and Ben-Hur found that *children of very strict, authoritarian parents were more likely to grow up pessimistic*, whereas *children of more permissive parents tended to be optimistic* . Strict environments often focus on what's wrong (criticism, punishment) rather than what's possible, potentially ingraining a negative bias. Permissive or at least flexible environments might allow children to see the world as a place where good things happen and mistakes aren't the end of the world.

In leadership terms, an optimistic leader often exudes confidence and can inspire a team with vision and positivity – but might underestimate risks. A pessimistic leader may excel at risk management and realism – but might demotivate the team or hesitate to seize opportunities . Both orientations have upsides and downsides . What's vital is being aware of your own tilt and balancing it. If you know you skew pessimistic (perhaps you recognize a voice of worry that sounds like a parent or your own childhood survival strategy), you can intentionally solicit positive viewpoints from others or practice reframing negative thoughts. If you skew overly optimistic (maybe you were shielded from hardship as a kid and always assume things will work out), you can train yourself to do a "worst-case scenario" check or appoint a trusted skeptic on your team to temper plans with realism.

A leader's default under pressure tends to revert to these learned outlooks . That's why one of the strategies we'll see in Part III for managing under pressure is to *consciously do the opposite of your tendency* (e.g., an optimist deliberately looks for potential problems; a pessimist asks, "What could go right here?")

Developing this skill can make you a more balanced decision-maker. But it starts with recognizing where your baseline was set. Think back: were you an Eeyore or a Tigger as a child? What messages about hope or worry did you get from your family? Understanding that context can help you catch yourself in unhelpful thought patterns as a leader and adjust.

- Self-Regulation vs. Expression – How We Learned to Show (or Hide) Emotions: Emotional intelligence heavily involves self-regulation – the ability to manage one's emotional reactions – and empathy/ attunement to others' emotions. Both are profoundly influenced by childhood emotional education. Let's examine how a child's environment teaches them either to bottle emotions (internalize), to wear them on their sleeve (externalize), or ideally to express them in healthy ways.

From a young age, children get feedback, explicit or implicit, about their emotional expressions. Some key patterns identified in research :

High-Emotion Environments: If you grew up in a household where emotions ran high—perhaps frequent fights, loud reactions, or drama—you might have been constantly triggered and thus more likely to become an externalizer (someone who openly shows emotions). Children in such environments learn that big emotions are the norm . As a leader, an externalizer might be passionate and energetic, able to rally people with enthusiasm (that's a plus), but also might let stress and anger spill over, affecting others negatively. For example, a leader who had a very volatile home life may unconsciously replicate that by having a short fuse at work or reacting strongly to news, good or bad. It feels natural to them to respond with intensity, because that was their baseline growing up.

Parental Modeling: Children mimic how parents express feelings. If your parents were emotionally expressive—laughing, crying, yelling when upset—you likely grew up comfortable showing emotion. If your parents were stoic and rarely showed emotion, you might have learned to keep feelings inside . Fast forward to leadership: a person who never saw their father cry or their mother express anger might struggle with identifying their own emotions or feel it's "unprofessional" to show any emotion at work. They could come off as distant or hard to read (akin to the avoidant attachment from last chapter). Conversely, someone who observed a lot of emotional openness might be more empathetic and quick to notice others' feelings, which is great, but might need to ensure they moderate their own expressions to not overwhelm others.

Reactions to Child's Emotions: This is crucial. If as a child you were comforted when you were upset, you learned it's okay to feel and that feelings can be managed . If your emotions were *ignored*, you might have learned to amplify them to be heard (which can create an externalizer: "I must cry louder to get attention"). If your emotions were *punished or shamed*, you likely became an internalizer: "Showing emotion gets me in trouble, better to hide it" . Kinley's research noted that children whose parents *minimized or ignored* their emotions tend to become externalizers (perhaps because they keep escalating emotional displays hoping someone will notice), whereas those whose parents *scolded or punished* emotional expression tend to become internalizers. Think about that: were you ever told "Stop crying or I'll give you something to cry about" or perhaps teased for being afraid? Those messages have a lasting impact. An internalizer leader often remains *cool and composed* under pressure (a useful trait) but may also *struggle to recognize and address emotions in their team* (a drawback) . They might miss signs of burnout or frustration in employees because they themselves have learned to suppress such signals. An externalizer leader might be very quick to react and share their feelings, which can be authentic and inspiring, but might also cause them to act impulsively or not filter emotional responses when it would be wise to do so.

Emotional Coaching: Some parents actively help children understand their feelings ("I see you're angry because your toy broke; it's okay to feel mad, let's figure out what to do") . This is gold in developing emotional intelligence. Children who receive this kind of coaching tend to handle emotions better as adults . They have a vocabulary for feelings and know some strategies to cope (because someone taught them, e.g., taking deep breaths, talking it out). In leadership, these individuals are often self-aware and composed, and also good at helping their teams navigate emotional moments (like calming tensions in a meeting, or encouraging a stressed employee to take a pause). If you didn't get this coaching as a kid, fear not – you can coach yourself now, or seek mentors and resources to learn the skills. We'll be covering several techniques in later chapters (like reframing stressful situations and using a trigger management plan).

To visualize these ideas, many experts refer to the "recognition vs. regulation" matrix of emotional competence:

	Recognition	Regulation
Personal Competence	**Self-Awareness** • Self-confidence • Awareness of your emotional state • Recognizing how your behavior impacts others • Paying attention to how others influence your emotional state	**Self-Management** • Keeping disruptive emotions and impulses in check • Acting in congruence with your values • Handling change flexibly • Pursuing goals and opportunities despite obstacles and setbacks
Social Competence	**Social Awareness** • Picking up on the mood in the room • Caring what others are going through • Hearing what the other person is "really" saying	**Relationship Management** • Getting along well with others • Handling conflict effectively • Clearly expressing ideas/information • Using sensitivity to another person's feeling (empathy) to manage interactions successfully

Figure: The Domains of Emotional Intelligence. On the "Recognition" side (seeing what's happening), we have Self-Awareness *(knowing one's own emotions) and* Social Awareness *(empathy for others' emotions). On the "Regulation" side (responding effectively), we have* Self-Management *(controlling one's emotions and impulses) and* Relationship Management *(handling interpersonal interactions, conflict, leadership). Childhood strongly influences the development of each quadrant – a supportive upbringing often yields higher self and social awareness, while practice and coaching foster better self and relationship management.*

In the figure above, think about your childhood influence on each quadrant:

Self-Awareness: Did your upbringing encourage you to notice and name your feelings? For example, "You seem sad – want to talk about it?" If yes, you likely have an edge in self-awareness (you can tell when you're frustrated, or nervous, etc., which is crucial as a leader). If not, you may sometimes feel upset or off without knowing why, which complicates things like decision-making. But you can improve self-awareness with journaling or therapy or even simple check-ins with yourself during the day ("What am I feeling right now and why?"). Leaders with strong self-awareness are more self-confident and realistic about their abilities – they know their strengths and limits. For example, a self-aware leader might think, "I'm feeling overwhelmed by this project, and I know I tend to snap at people when stressed. Let me delegate some tasks and take a short break." Someone with low self-awareness might just start snapping and not realize stress is the driver.

Self-Management: As a child, were you taught ways to soothe yourself when upset? Maybe a parent modeled taking deep breaths or calmly troubleshooting a problem. Or were you left to flounder? Self-management in adulthood – keeping disruptive emotions in check, maintaining integrity under pressure, being adaptable – has roots in those early practices . Ravi's story is instructive here: he had been a *sickly child* whom doctors advised to avoid exertion, but he defied that limitation and played sports under a mentor's guidance . Through that process, he learned *resilience* and not to be ruled by fear. As a leader, Ravi later emphasized making decisions even without all data, trusting his resilience and encouraging his team to face fears rather than avoid them . He effectively learned and taught self-management of fear. If you find you struggle with impulses (like firing off angry emails or panicking in a crunch), it might be that you didn't get to internalize those calming strategies early on. But you can start practicing now – one simple method is the 10-second rule (take ten seconds before reacting to anything emotional). Also, remind yourself of values: self- management often means acting in congruence with your values, not your momentary feelings.

If "respect" is a value, let it guide you in a heated moment rather than anger.

Social Awareness (Empathy): Were you taught to consider others' feelings as a child? Maybe through religion, or by parents pointing out, "Look, your friend is sad because you took his toy"? That builds empathy. Children who have secure attachments and whose feelings were respected usually develop better empathy. Also, having diverse social interactions in childhood (e.g., being in team sports, clubs, or a big family like Sangeetha's) can improve social awareness because you see more perspectives. A socially aware leader can "read the room," pick up on team morale, sense when someone is bothered even if not said outright. If you feel you're not great at this, don't label yourself a lost cause; empathy can be improved by active listening and simply paying attention. One tip is to observe body language and tone in meetings more consciously. Challenge yourself: next meeting, try to identify how each person might be feeling (even jot words like "engaged," "skeptical," "hesitant") purely by observation. You might be surprised how this trains your awareness.

Relationship Management: This is the capstone – using awareness of emotions (yours and others') to manage interactions successfully. It includes clear communication, effective conflict management, inspiring and influencing others, teamwork – in essence, leadership itself. Childhood experiences like handling sibling rivalry, or negotiating with parents for a later bedtime, even playground leadership in games, all provide early practice in these skills. Some children get explicit teaching (e.g., "Use your words, not fists" or being assigned roles that build leadership), while others learn the hard way or not at all. If as a child you often felt misunderstood or failed in social situations, you might enter adulthood with some deficits in these skills. But every leader can consciously improve them. For example, conflict resolution can be learned via workshops or mentors if you didn't pick it up earlier. One leader I know, who grew up in a very conflict-avoidant family (everything was swept under the rug), struggled immensely the first time he had to fire someone he literally felt ill. He sought guidance and realized he had to develop a new script for conflict: one that saw it as sometimes necessary and even beneficial. With coaching, he learned techniques to manage tough conversations (like sticking to facts, expressing empathy but not backing down from the message). Over time, he became much more adept at difficult but crucial aspects of leadership relationship management.

The connection between childhood and emotional intelligence is perhaps most vividly seen when leaders are under *stress*. Recall from earlier the concept of internalizers vs. externalizers under pressure. Internalizers (often avoidant types) focus and seem calm but may suppress valuable input from their emotions or fail to empathize with stressed team members. Externalizers (often anxious or just expressive types) bring energy and can voice intuitive hunches, but risk being governed by their feelings and transmitting their anxiety or anger to others. Neither is purely good or bad. The ideal is to find a middle ground: *controlled expression*. Leaders who master this can be emotionally authentic (they don't come off as robots) yet emotionally intelligent (they don't dump their raw emotions on others or make rash decisions). If you reflect on your upbringing, you might find clues: did you learn *self-control* or *self- expression* more? Often people have to strengthen the opposite muscle in adulthood. A leader from a very stoic background might practice sharing more ("I admit I'm disappointed by these results, but here's how we can improve..." – a bit of feeling plus solution). A leader from a very emotionally volatile background might practice pausing and filtering ("I'm furious right now, but let me hold that for a second and speak to what we need to do").

Bringing in a practical example from the interviews: Michelle noted that in her coaching, women leaders were often more willing to explore how childhood shaped their emotional responses, whereas men were sometimes less inclined . This could be due to cultural conditioning: many boys are taught to downplay emotion. As a result, some male leaders (not all, of course) might reach mid-career having rarely examined their emotional landscape, which can be a blind spot. Michelle's advice to all leaders is to seek feedback and cultivate self-awareness early , precisely so that these blind spots in emotional intelligence can be addressed before they derail someone (like the classic scenario of the brilliant executive who lacks "people skills" and thus cannot lead effectively). The fact that her male and female clients differed in willingness to introspect is itself a childhood artifact of gender norms. So if you find yourself resistant to this "soft stuff," consider that perhaps you were simply never given permission to delve into it – and give yourself that permission now, as a strategic move to improve your leadership.

Building Emotional Intelligence Going Forward: Recognizing childhood's role is step one. Step two is actively developing your EI competencies. We will cover a lot of these strategies in Part III (Chapter 10 specifically focuses on growing emotional intelligence and resilience), but as a preview, here are a few things you can start even as you reflect on your early emotional lessons:

- *Name Your Emotions:* This sounds simple, but many people struggle to precisely identify what they feel (e.g., distinguishing anger from anxiety from shame). As the old adage goes, "Name it to tame it." Practice expanding your emotional vocabulary. Instead of just "I feel bad" try "I feel anxious/ nervous about the upcoming deadline because I fear we might miss it." Encourage your team to do the same in appropriate settings. This practice may counteract a childhood where emotions were not discussed. It activates your prefrontal brain (logical part) to manage the limbic feelings.
- *Reframe Negative Thoughts:* If you notice pessimistic or catastrophic thinking (perhaps echoing a parent's voice from childhood), challenge it. For instance, turn "This project is ruined; I've failed" into "This project's outcome is disappointing, but one setback doesn't equal total failure. What can we learn?" Reframing is a learned skill that some fortunate people pick up early (maybe they had an encouraging teacher or parent), but anyone can learn it later too. We'll practice this more later.
- *Breathing and Grounding Techniques:* Remember how you might have been taught as a kid to "take a deep breath" when upset? If you weren't, teach yourself now. Deep, slow breathing actually signals the

body to calm down. Some leaders use a technique like box breathing (inhale 4 seconds, hold 4, exhale 4, hold 4) in stressful meetings or before speaking. Grounding means focusing on the present physical moment (like feeling your feet on the floor) to avoid being swept away by emotion. These simple tools can re-regulate an agitated nervous system – something a supportive caregiver might have done by holding a child's hand. Now you can figuratively hold your own hand through self-soothing strategies.

- *Cultivate Empathy via Curiosity:* If empathy wasn't your household's strong suit growing up, you can nurture it now by simple curiosity. Make it a habit to ask people open-ended questions and really listen. For instance, if a team member's performance has slipped, instead of assuming they're lazy or don't care, curiously inquire, "I've noticed a change in your work lately. How are you feeling about everything? Is there anything affecting you that I should know about?" This not only gives you insight (maybe they have a personal issue or are feeling burned out), it also signals you care. Often that alone boosts their engagement. Curiosity is a bridge to empathy. As you hear others' experiences, you naturally broaden your understanding of emotions beyond your own perspective.

By examining how your childhood taught you (or didn't teach you) about emotions, you gain a clear starting point for improving your emotional intelligence as a leader. It's like knowing your baseline in a fitness program – if you know you can currently jog 1 km without stopping (or maybe you can barely jog at all), you can set training goals from there. Similarly, if you discover, "I tend to shut down when conflict arises" (perhaps a result of childhood patterns), you can specifically work on conflict navigation skills. Or if you realize "I get disproportionately upset when my authority is questioned" (maybe an old wound of feeling disrespected in youth), you can acknowledge that and practice more measured responses.

In the next chapter, Chapter 4, we will turn to the realm of beliefs and schemas – the cognitive frameworks born in childhood that influence our leadership decisions and interpretations. Before moving on, take a moment to jot down: *What's one emotional pattern I recognize in myself that likely has early origins?* It could be "I don't cry in front of others" or "I always expect disaster if something goes wrong" or "I raise my voice without realizing it when I'm passionate." With that insight, you're already ahead of the game. Emotional self-awareness is the first component of emotional intelligence, and as Goleman notes, it's the foundation for all the rest . You are building that foundation brick by brick, using memories and reflections from long ago to create a sturdier, wiser structure for the future.

CHAPTER 4

THE STORIES WE TELL OURSELVES – CHILDHOOD BELIEFS AND LEADERSHIP SCHEMA

When Malik, a regional sales director, was offered a promotion to a national role, he hesitated. On paper he was the perfect candidate, yet something held him back. In a candid conversation with a mentor, Malik admitted, "I'm not sure I'm cut out for the big leagues. I come from a tiny town; people like me don't end up in corner offices." Hearing those words aloud surprised even him. Where had that thought come from? Malik's mentor gently pointed out that his track record disproved that belief—he had delivered stellar results for years. They dug deeper and uncovered the source: growing up, Malik had rarely seen anyone from his community rise to top corporate ranks, and an offhand comment by a high school teacher ("Don't aim too high, be practical") had lodged in his mind. Unknowingly, Malik was carrying a *schema*—a core belief—that people of his background couldn't succeed at that level. It wasn't true, but it felt true, and it was almost enough to stop him from seizing a real opportunity. This is the power of the stories we tell ourselves, many of which originate in childhood. In this chapter, we'll examine how early experiences form our fundamental beliefs (and misbeliefs) about ourselves and how these *schemas* influence our leadership behavior and decisions. More importantly, we'll look at how to identify and begin to change the narratives that limit us.

What Are Schemas? In psychology, a schema is an enduring belief or framework through which we view the world, often formed in childhood or adolescence. You can think of it as a lens that colors every experience. Schemas answer basic questions like: *Am I competent or inadequate? Can I trust others or will they betray me? Am I worthy of love and respect, or do I have to earn it through achievement?* These beliefs often start as coping mechanisms or interpretations of childhood events. A child who is constantly criticized may develop a schema of "I'm not good enough." One who had to care for younger siblings might form "I must always be responsible for others." These schemas usually feel entirely normal to the person – as Monica Johnson, Psy.D., notes, the ideology may feel "entirely ordinary" because it's been part of you for so long.

Schemas are self-perpetuating and resistant to change ; we tend to interpret new experiences in ways that confirm them. For example, if Malik had a "I'm not cut out for big roles" schema, even after many successes he might attribute them to luck or think "Well, that was just a fluke, the national role is different." We all have schemas – some positive, some negative. The negative ones, often called "early maladaptive schemas" in schema therapy, can seriously undermine leadership effectiveness if not addressed.

Leadership amplifies the impact of schemas. When a schema is triggered, a leader can shift into a mode of behavior that is more about their own inner narrative than about the reality of the situation. Psychologist Jeffrey Young identified common schemas (like Defectiveness, Abandonment, Unrelenting Standards, etc.) and how people develop coping styles around them – some overcompensate, some surrender, some avoid. Let's look at a few examples that frequently appear in leadership contexts:

- *Impostor Syndrome (Defectiveness Schema):* This is the feeling of being a fraud, that you're not as capable as others think. It often comes from a schema Young would call *Defectiveness/Inadequacy* – a belief formed perhaps by overly critical parents or a childhood where love was conditional on achievement. As a leader, this schema might cause you to overwork and micromanage (to hide your perceived flaws), struggle to accept praise, or avoid high-visibility opportunities for fear of being "exposed." I have observed that some of my coaching clients, especially those who had very high expectations placed on them by family, carried an internal critic always saying "not good enough." They had to learn to recognize that voice as an echo of the past, not an accurate evaluation of their present skills.

"I must do it all" (Unrelenting Standards & Vulnerability Schemas): Some leaders believe they must be the first in and last out, shouldering every burden. This can spring from an *Unrelenting Standards* schema (perfectionism) often rooted in childhood where praise came only when one was the best, or mistakes were harshly punished. It can also tie to a *Vulnerability* schema – a belief that if they rely on others, everything will collapse. Vasuta's early experience as the responsible eldest child gave her a strong responsibility schema . She believed "If I don't handle it, others will drop the ball." This made her a very dependable leader, but also led to burnout and a team that wasn't growing under her, because she wouldn't delegate . She eventually recognized that holding too much responsibility was limiting her effectiveness as a leader and depriving her team of growth . She had to unlearn that childhood lesson and replace it with a new narrative: "I am responsible for the team's outcomes, but that includes empowering them to take responsibility themselves." She started

to delegate more and saw her team thrive—an example of rewriting a schema-driven behavior.

- *Distrust (Abandonment/Mistrust Schema):* If a leader deep down believes "people will hurt or abandon me" (perhaps due to early loss or betrayal), they may have a hard time building close working relationships. They might keep a certain distance, or become overly controlling to ensure no one can let them down. This schema can cause them to read malicious intent where there is none, or to be reluctant to mentor others ("why invest if they'll just leave?"). A distrustful leader might also inadvertently create a self-fulfilling prophecy by alienating people with their lack of trust, thus people do become less loyal over time. Contrast that with someone who has a *secure/trust* schema from childhood: they generally assume good intent and find it easier to collaborate and delegate trustfully. Leaders can move toward trust by slowly taking measured risks in relying on others and seeing positive results, gradually disconfirming the old belief.

Need for Approval (Approval-Seeking Schema): Some leaders are overly concerned with being liked and approved of. This might come from a childhood schema that love = approval. They might avoid giving tough feedback or making unpopular but necessary decisions, hurting the organization in the long run. Sangeetha mentioned how one of her clients had to break his limiting belief about communication stemming from schooling background . Part of that was an approval issue—he felt he needed to speak "perfect English" to be respected. By highlighting his actual successes and strengths, Sangeetha helped him see he already had others' respect; he could drop the anxious approval-seeking and focus on authentic communication. In leadership, excessive approval- seeking can lead to indecisiveness (trying to please everyone) and loss of respect (if you bend with every wind of opinion). Recognizing this schema can be the first step to prioritize *respect over popularity* – ironically leading to greater respect and trust from others in the end.

Schemalike beliefs can operate beneath awareness until we *name them*. A fantastic exercise is to fill in the blank: "As a leader, I am _**" or "A good leader must _**". Write whatever comes out, without overthinking. You might get answers like "I am only as good as my last success" or "must never show weakness" or "should always have the answer". Once these statements are visible, ask "Where might this belief come from?" Perhaps "I'm only as good as my achievements" echoes a childhood where love was performance-based. Or "never show weakness" might have been a survival rule if you grew up in a tough neighborhood or strict household.

Blind Spots from Childhood Beliefs: These schemas often create *blind spots* – things about ourselves we cannot see but others can. In leadership terms, a blind spot might be a behavior or assumption that is limiting you, but you're not aware of it. Many blind spots are essentially schema-driven. In Chapter 6 (upcoming) we'll discuss the Johari Window: the "Blind spot" quadrant is what others see but you don't. For example, a leader with a *defectiveness schema* might not realize how often they downplay their accomplishments and how that undermines their credibility (others see someone who oddly doesn't project confidence, even though they have every reason to). Or a leader with a *mistrust schema* might not see how their micromanaging signals "I don't trust you" to the team, even as they justify it to themselves as "being thorough." These are blind spots rooted in internal narratives. We'll explore tools like feedback to uncover blind spots in Part II, but it's worth noting here how intertwined beliefs and blind spots are. Robert Kegan, a developmental psychologist, talks about "subject vs object" – when a belief is *subject*, it owns you; when you can see it as *object*, you own it. We want to turn our subjectively held childhood beliefs into objective things we can examine and change.

Changing the Script: Perhaps the most important takeaway is that *schemas are not destiny*. Once you identify a limiting narrative, you can *rewrite* it. This is akin to narrative therapy: viewing your life as a story where you are the author, not just a character being swept along. In fact, one study on executives found that those who actively reframed their personal narratives around challenges became more effective leaders – they saw themselves not as victims of circumstance but as learners and protagonists in control of their story. We see this in Harjeet's reflection: he went from a small-town boy who thought becoming a professor was the ceiling, to someone who, thanks to new experiences (engineering college, working at a big company), allowed himself to dream bigger . He consciously expanded his schema of what was possible: small-town dreams gave way to *big vision*. Now as a leader, when team members voice self-doubt or limited aspirations, Harjeet encourages them to challenge those assumptions, sharing his own journey of overcoming a limiting belief .

We will devote Chapter 9 entirely to the process of *rewriting your leadership narrative*, with frameworks and exercises to do so. But even here, let's touch on some strategies to start challenging limiting beliefs:

- Collect Evidence Against the Limiting Belief: Treat it like a hypothesis rather than truth. Malik, for instance, could list his accomplishments that counter "people like me can't succeed" – e.g., "I have been promoted three times, I've led successful projects, I have endorsements from senior leaders." Writing these down helps weaken the schema's hold. The schema feels *true*, but evidence shows it's not. This cognitive-behavioral approach can literally rewire your thought patterns over time.
- Seek New Experiences: If your schema says "I'm not a people person" because maybe you were shy as a kid, deliberately put yourself in situations to disconfirm that (like leading a volunteer group or running

a workshop). Positive experiences are the most powerful way to update beliefs. It might be uncomfortable at first (schemas resist change), but once you accumulate a few "Hey, I handled that social situation well" experiences, the belief will start to crumble.

- Mentorship and Role Models: Find leaders who share a similar background or challenge but clearly overcame it. For instance, if you're a woman in tech with an unconscious belief "I won't be taken seriously," look to trailblazers like Padmasree Warrior or Fei-Fei Li who carved paths in that field. Hearing their stories and advice can help rewrite your own. Or more directly, have a mentor who recognizes your schemas and nudges you when you're falling into old patterns. A mentor can often see your blind spots better than you can and can challenge statements like "Maybe I was just lucky" with "No, you earned it, and here's why."
- Narrative Reframing: This is a powerful exercise: Write a narrative of a pivotal leadership challenge you faced from a negative angle ("I failed because I'm not good at X..." etc.). Then rewrite it from a growth angle, focusing on what you learned and how you overcame or will overcome ("Though the project failed, I learned X and now I approach things differently, which has led to success in Y"). This helps break the identification with failure or weakness as a permanent state. It's essentially practicing seeing yourself as the *hero* of the story, not the victim. We often don't realize we have been telling, in our mind, a story where we're somehow not the hero. Change that script.
- Affirmations and New Beliefs: Identify a new, healthier belief you want to adopt and use it as a replacement whenever the old one surfaces. For example, an executive with a "I must be perfect" schema might adopt "I grow and innovate through my mistakes; perfection is not the goal, learning is." It might feel forced at first, but each time the anxiety of imperfection arises, consciously invoke the new belief. Over time, it sticks more. Similarly, "I'm not good enough" can be countered with

"I have strengths and I'm improving in areas of weakness; I am enough as a person regardless of outcomes." These are not cheesy platitudes – they are re-training your brain. Many highly successful leaders practice such reframing internally, turning inner critics into inner coaches.

We should also acknowledge that some schemas are rooted in childhood trauma or deep pain. For instance, a leader who was abused or lost a parent early may have an Abandonment or Abuse schema ("Everyone will leave me" or "People will hurt me"). These can profoundly affect personal and professional life. In such cases, professional therapy is often invaluable. It's not separate from leadership development; it *is* leadership development to heal those wounds. A healed leader can lead without projecting past pain onto current situations. One leader I worked with had a history of childhood abuse and realized he had unconsciously modeled his own management style on his abusive parent – harsh, arbitrary, intolerant of dissent. It was a shocking realization for him. Through therapy and coaching, he gradually transformed his style, incorporating empathy and patience that he had to learn afresh (since he'd never seen it at home). His team's performance and loyalty skyrocketed once he made these changes. It was a stark example of how confronting a childhood demon directly led to better leadership and business outcomes.

Finally, let's revisit the two leaders from the schema therapy article we mentioned: Paul (the volatile CEO) and Daniel (the approval-seeking VP). Both were operating in the "shadow of their schemas" : Paul's anger and bullying left his team walking on eggshells, likely stemming from a schema of entitlement or "I must always be right" – perhaps an overcompensation for insecurity. Daniel's constant need for approval made him ineffective in asserting ideas. Recognizing these patterns, they worked (with schema-trained coaches) to change. For someone like Paul, that likely meant learning humility and emotional regulation – possibly uncovering a childhood where he only got attention by being loud or "right." For Daniel, it meant building self-worth independent of others' praise. The article noted that these maladaptive schemas, when triggered, shift leaders into self-defeating behaviors . Our aim is to catch the shift *before* it derails us. By bringing your schemas from the shadows into the light, you regain choice.

As we conclude Part I, we have covered the foundational influences: relationships (attachment), emotional patterns (emotional intelligence), and core beliefs (schemas). These are the pillars constructed in childhood that hold up, for better or worse, the edifice of your leadership style. You might be reflecting that *some* of your pillars are rock solid and have been strengths (maybe a parent instilled a love of learning, and now you excel at strategic thinking), while *others* might be cracked or misaligned (maybe fear was a constant in childhood, and now you avoid necessary risks). The next step in this journey is to excavate – to dig into your own life story and bring those influences fully into awareness. With understanding in hand, we will then move to transform what needs changing. Part II is all about that self-discovery process: the tools and experiences to uncover your inner child's impact on your current self. It may be at times an emotional archaeology, but remember: the goal is not to dwell in the past, it's to free yourself from its unseen constraints and reclaim the gifts it offers. As the saying goes, "The truth will set you free." In leadership, the truths of your childhood can indeed set you free to become the most authentic and effective leader you can be—once you have the courage to face them. Let's begin that excavation.

Leadership Pulse

Insights gathered from a leadership survey conducted across 600 leaders in the US, Europe, APAC, and India.

Section 1: Understanding the Connection

1. How strongly do you believe childhood experiences influence leadership development?

Region	Strongly	Moderately	Slightly	Not at all
US	48%	38%	11%	3%
Europe	51%	33%	13%	3%
APAC	61%	27%	10%	2%
India	69%	22%	8%	1%
Global Avg	57%	30%	10.5%	2.5%

Insight: Most leaders, especially in India and APAC, believe that early life experiences significantly shape leadership capabilities.

2. Which childhood factors have the most impact on leadership styles?

Region	Top 1 Factor	Top 2 Factor
US	Family dynamics	Social interactions with peers
Europe	Family dynamics	Early education experiences
APAC	Family dynamics	Cultural/societal norms
India	Family dynamics	Cultural/societal norms

Insight: Family dynamics are universally seen as critical, with cultural norms playing a major role in APAC and India.

3. Can you recall a specific childhood experience that influenced how you lead or make decisions today?

Open-ended Themes Identified Globally:

- Parental role modeling / emotional neglect → shaped empathy or need for validation
- Early responsibility (e.g., caregiving, earning) → developed resilience and ownership

- Bullying or peer exclusion → enhanced conflict sensitivity or led to people-pleasing behaviors
- Academic pressure or performance comparison → cultivated perfectionism or drive

Section 2: Impact on Leadership Style

4. Which leadership qualities do you feel are most shaped by early experiences?

Leadership Quality	% Chosen
Empathy and emotional intelligence	71%
Decision-making under pressure	48%
Conflict resolution and negotiation	45%
Vision-setting and inspiration	32%

Insight: Empathy and emotional intelligence were cited as most influenced by early experiences.

5. How do you think your childhood influenced your approach to building and managing teams?
Top Thematic Responses:
- Tendency to over-manage from environments where mistakes weren't tolerated
- Active listening developed from being ignored as a child
- Early responsibility leading to strong ownership
- Conflict avoidance from growing up in high-conflict households

6. Have you ever reflected on your childhood to understand your leadership behaviors?

Region	Yes, frequently	Occasionally	Rarely	Never
US	29%	42%	21%	8%
Europe	25%	48%	22%	5%
APAC	34%	39%	20%	7%
India	41%	38%	17%	4%
Global Avg	32%	42%	20%	6%

Insight: 74% of global leaders have reflected on childhood in relation to leadership behaviors.

Section 3: Overcoming Limiting Beliefs

7. Do you feel any beliefs or behaviors developed in childhood have limited your effectiveness as a leader?

Region	Yes	No	Not sure
US	54%	28%	18%
Europe	48%	33%	19%
APAC	62%	23%	15%
India	68%	21%	11%
Global Avg	58%	26%	16%

Insight: Over half of leaders recognize limiting beliefs from childhood still affect leadership performance.

Conclusion

This survey confirms that:

- **Childhood is not just personal history—it's leadership context.**
- Leaders across all regions, especially in India and APAC, deeply associate **early life narratives** with how they lead today.
- Emotional traits like empathy and behavioral patterns like control or perfectionism often have **childhood roots**.
- A growing number of leaders are **reflecting on childhood** to enhance leadership effectiveness, supporting the transformational pathway described in *The Leader Was Once a Child*

PART II

EXCAVATION – UNEARTHING YOUR INNER FOUNDATIONS

In Part II, we turn inward. Having established that childhood experiences profoundly influence leadership behavior, we now focus on discovering your specific influences. These four chapters serve as a guide for self- exploration. You will create your personal leadership timeline, identify hidden blind spots, recognize emotional triggers rooted in your past, and begin the process of healing and reframing those childhood-derived patterns. This is the introspective heart of the book – where awareness is sharpened and insights emerge. By courageously digging into your own story, you prepare the ground for meaningful change in Part III.

CHAPTER 5

DIGGING FOR GOLD – DISCOVERING YOUR LEADERSHIP STORY

A seasoned executive once said, "I've had 30 years of experience – or 1 year of experience repeated 30 times." What makes the difference between those who simply accumulate years in leadership and those who truly grow and evolve is self-reflection. Self-reflection is how we extract wisdom from experience. In this chapter, we'll embark on a reflective exercise to excavate the layers of your life and find the formative experiences that shaped your leadership approach. Think of it as constructing a Leadership Timeline – a personal history of events, big and small, that left an imprint on how you lead today. We are digging for gold nuggets of insight: perhaps an early success that gave you confidence (a "gold star" moment), or a painful failure that taught you caution (a "scar" moment). We'll also gather input from others as needed, like archaeologists consulting local lore, to make sure we don't miss blind spots. The goal is to gain a narrative understanding of your leadership development so far, connecting childhood, adolescence, early career, and current day. Once you see the storyline, you can better edit it in the future.

Plotting Your Leadership Timeline: A useful tool here is to literally draw a timeline. Take a horizontal line across a page, mark one end as birth (or earliest childhood memory) and the other end as today. Now start marking points for significant moments related to leadership, character, or turning points in your life. Some prompts to identify those points:

Early Childhood: What is your first memory of "leadership" or responsibility? Maybe it's organizing a game in the playground, or standing up for a friend being bullied, or even being put in charge of a younger sibling for the first time. How did it make you feel? Harjeet, for example, remembered running a little summer coaching class with friends as a teenager, which taught him about investing in relationships and trust . That's a golden nugget: it showed him early that leadership involves earning trust by caring. Mark such memories down.

Adolescence: The teenage years often offer formative leadership experiences (being a team captain, a camp counselor, leading a school project) *or* experiences of being led (a teacher or coach who influenced you). Did you have an empowering mentor or a toxic one? How did that shape your idea of leadership? Sangeetha's co-ed school experience during this period, where she faced naysayers and had to prove herself, is a key plot point on her timeline that fueled her drive . On your timeline, note any pivotal challenge or success in high school or college that might have nudged your path – maybe running for student council (and winning, or losing), or deciding *not* to go for a leadership role because of self-doubt (that too is informative: what held you back?).

- *Early Career:* Your first jobs often cast leadership in a new light. You encounter workplace hierarchies, office politics, teamwork beyond the classroom. Think of your first boss – what did you learn from them about leadership (even if by negative example)? Did you step up in a project and get recognition, or shy away from taking charge? Mark significant moments, like the first time you managed someone (even informally) or a project where you took the lead. Ravi admitted he hadn't thought about childhood influences until much later , but one could imagine his rebellious teen streak (challenging the status quo) carried into how he approached innovative projects early in his career . Plot those traits and see if the line connecting from youth to first jobs is clear.

Personal Life Milestones: Leadership isn't only shaped at work. Major life events – moving countries, losing a loved one, becoming a parent – affect how we lead. If you moved around a lot as a kid, maybe you became good at adapting (or maybe you hate change to this day – either insight is valuable). If you faced economic hardship growing up, maybe you developed grit and resourcefulness that serve you in business, or perhaps a scarcity mindset that now influences how you manage budgets and risk. Note on the timeline events like "family moved when I was 8 – felt uprooted" or "age 16, parents divorced – had to become the peacemaker for siblings." Draw lines or arrows to how these might correlate with leadership tendencies (e.g., "peacemaker at home -> now often mediate conflicts at work"). Michelle mentioned birth order and family climate as key influences – mark your birth order and any notable dynamics (like "as middle child, learned to negotiate," etc.).

- *Key Triumphs and Trials:* Identify two or three high points (successes) and low points (failures or crises) in your leadership journey so far. A high point could be "Led my team to exceed targets by 50% in 2019" or "Successfully navigated the team through a sudden budget cut." Low might be "Botched an important presentation" or "Conflict in team caused two people to quit." For each, reflect: what personal qualities or behaviors led to those outcomes? Do they trace back to earlier experiences? For instance, a leader who saved a project by working 80-hour weeks might realize that behavior stems from a childhood belief that hard work equals worth (it yielded success but at what personal cost?). Or a leader whose team had a conflict might trace their own mishandling of it to never having seen healthy conflict resolution growing up. These incidents are rich learning material – mark them and write a sentence of what you learned or could have learned from each.

Now that you have a timeline with various marks, look for patterns and cause-effect links. Do you see a thread from childhood to now? Sometimes it helps to use different colors or symbols for themes. You might circle all events that boosted your confidence in one color, and those that undermined it in another. Or tag events with labels like [Trust], [Conflict], [Risk-taking], [Self-belief]. This thematic view can reveal, for example, that many of your confidence boosts came from solo achievements, whereas team experiences maybe were more mixed – which might suggest you're more comfortable relying on yourself (perhaps due to childhood solo sports vs team sports or such). Or you might notice that every time you had a micromanaging boss you clashed – which might connect to an authority schema from childhood (maybe you rebel against strict authority thanks to a controlling parent or conversely, you can't stand not being in control due to that).

Life Narrative Exercise: Another approach (particularly if timelines aren't your thing) is to write a short narrative of your life focusing on leadership-related moments. Write it like a story, maybe a page or two, starting with "Once there was a child who…" and ending with "…and that child grew up to be a leader who…". It sounds a bit whimsical, but writing in the third person can provide distance and insight. For example: "Once there was a child who loved organizing her friends to put on little plays. She felt joy in bringing people together to create something fun. But when she entered middle school, a popular girl laughed at one of her ideas in front of everyone. The child felt embarrassed and decided it was safer not to lead openly. Years later, as a young manager, she found herself holding back in meetings, a little of that old fear still whispering in her ear…" and so on. By narrating it, you may see the continuity that "whispering fear" from childhood is still present. The narrative can then pivot: "...One day, she realized that the fear was a voice from the past, not the present. She began to speak up more, little by little, reclaiming the joy she once had in rallying people together." This type of story-making helps consolidate your reflections into a meaningful context. It moves you from a list of events to an understanding of who you are becoming as a leader and why.

Seeking External Reflections: Excavation isn't a solo job; sometimes you need additional perspectives. This is where feedback and conversations come in. Identify a few people who know you well (trusted colleagues, friends, family) and ask them questions that might uncover things you can't see. For example:

- "What do you think are some of my strongest traits as a leader, and where do you think those come from in my personality or background?"
- "Have you noticed any situations that really throw me off balance or push my buttons?" (This might highlight a trigger you hadn't articulated. A friend might say, "Yeah, you really get upset when someone challenges your expertise in front of others," connecting maybe to an insecurity from younger days.)
- "If you had to tell a story about what made me the leader I am, what would you say?" (This is interesting because people often have narratives about us that we don't realize. Maybe your spouse says, "Oh, you've always been the responsible one since you were 10 and your mom was ill; that made you a natural caretaker leader." You might think, *Huh, I never considered that connection.*)

Be open when you ask – make it clear you're reflecting and not fishing for compliments. People might hesitate to be honest, so reassure them you truly want insight and you're not going to be defensive. When they respond, just listen and take notes. There might be gold in what they mention casually.

For instance, one leader did this exercise and a colleague reminded him of a project early in his career where he took an unconventional approach that succeeded. The colleague said, "I think that's when you became the risk-taker you are – management gave you praise for it, and you got hooked." The leader realized that indeed, being rewarded for smart risks early on gave him a bit of a daredevil style – generally good, but it also meant he sometimes took risks without adequate consultation, which had backfired a couple of times. That insight let him refine his approach: keep the courage, but add more team input to mitigate downsides.

Identify Your Leadership Anchors and Biases: As you compile your story, it helps to list a few key *anchors* (positive guiding beliefs) and *biases* (potentially limiting beliefs or blind spots) that emerge. Anchors might be "I believe in developing people (because my first boss believed in me)" or "I value transparency (because I grew up in an environment of secrecy that caused harm)." Biases could be "I tend to distrust senior management (perhaps because my father lost his job unexpectedly when I was young, making me cynical about higher-ups)" or "I assume conflict will destroy relationships (because my parents' fights led to divorce, so I avoid conflict)." Write these out. These are neither final verdicts nor excuses – they are working hypotheses about what shapes your instincts.

For example, if you write as a bias "I have trouble trusting others with critical tasks," you might trace it to an incident maybe where a classmate botched a team assignment when you were 12, and you got scolded for it. That stuck: "If I don't do it myself, I get let down." That's powerful to know! It doesn't mean that belief is correct in your 40-year-old professional life, but it means a part of you is acting on a 12-year-old's logic. Knowing that, you can actively update the logic (we'll do more in Part III, but you can start testing it by gradually delegating and gathering new evidence).

Case: Sangeetha's Reflection: Let's illustrate an excavation with Sangeetha's story. If she plotted her timeline, she'd mark growing up in a joint family learning adaptability, the co-ed challenge fueling competitive spirit, transitioning from CFO to entrepreneur which demanded questioning status quo beliefs, and coaching clients which gave her insight into how widespread limiting beliefs are. She might note a bias: "I tend to initially underestimate people who are too self-deprecating because I've seen so many with low confidence (like that client) – I might project my desire to help onto them even if they don't need it." And an anchor: "I strongly believe in relationship-first leadership (thanks Mom for teaching me win-win) ." With that self-awareness, Sangeetha can ensure her bias doesn't lead to micromanaging someone who just has a different style, and she can double down on her relationship strength to influence others.

Reflection and Journaling: This chapter itself is an exercise—there's no substitute for doing the writing or deep thinking. If you haven't started jotting down notes about your timeline or narrative while reading, consider taking some time now. We've provided the framework; the excavation won't happen just by reading – you have to dig. Journaling is a powerful way to continue this work. Some prompts to journal on:

- "One childhood experience that made me feel capable was... How does that still show up in my leadership?"
- "One childhood experience that made me feel afraid or inadequate was... How might that shadow still appear at work?"
- "Messages I got about authority (respecting or rebelling) as a kid included... Now, my relationship with authority (or how I wield authority) is..."
- "As a teenager, my biggest challenge was... and I coped by... Does a similar coping mechanism appear in my leadership today?"
- "People who have influenced my leadership style: [list]. What did each teach me (intentionally or unintentionally)?"

- "If my 10-year-old self saw me now, they'd be surprised that I …, and they'd probably tell me …." (This one's a bit imaginative – but it can yield insight. Maybe your 10-year-old self would say "Why do you worry so much about what others think? We used to just do stuff for fun!" – a reminder to not lose that spirit.)

Self-discovery is an ongoing process. You might find that once you "dig up" a memory or pattern, more things start making sense. It can be emotional – be prepared for that. Some people recall painful incidents they hadn't thought of in ages. If that happens, take care of yourself. It might even be worth discussing deep or painful discoveries with a therapist or a trusted confidant. Remember, the aim is constructive: to learn, not to wallow or assign blame. Approach your past with compassion for that younger you, and appreciation for how far you've come.

By the end of this excavation, you should have a clearer narrative of *why* you lead the way you do. For instance, you might realize, *"I'm a consensus-builder because I grew up mediating family disputes – it served me well, but sometimes I overdo it and avoid necessary decisive action."* That's a gold nugget of insight. Or, *"I always volunteer for the hardest tasks because I learned early that's how to stand out – but now it's burning me out; I need to let others share the load."* Another nugget.

Armed with these insights, we move to the next step: shining light on the unseen parts of ourselves that others may see – our blind spots. In Chapter 6, we'll use tools like the Johari Window and feedback techniques to uncover what might still be buried just outside our own view. Think of Chapter 5 as unearthing the artifacts and writing your site report, and Chapter 6 as bringing in extra floodlights to spot the things you might have missed and polish those artifacts. Each chapter builds on the last, so keep your timeline/narrative handy as we proceed. We'll keep referring to your discoveries as we tackle specific areas like blind spots, triggers, and healing old patterns.

You've begun the courageous work of self-excavation. It can be challenging, but remember the purpose: to liberate yourself from autopilot leadership and enable conscious, authentic leadership. Every insight is a step toward greater freedom and effectiveness. The leader who knows themselves can lead themselves – and others – anywhere. Let's continue that journey.

CHAPTER 6

FACING THE MIRROR – IDENTIFYING YOUR LEADERSHIP BLIND SPOTS

Midway through a leadership workshop, the facilitator asked everyone to write down a weakness that had been pointed out to them repeatedly in their career. Arjun, a high-performing marketing manager, confidently wrote "I care too much about excellence" (a polished way of saying *perfectionist* perhaps, which he already knew about himself). When it came time for peer feedback, however, one colleague gently added, "Sometimes you don't realize how your tone comes across as dismissive." Arjun was taken aback. Dismissive? Him? Others chimed in with hesitation: yes, at times he shut down ideas quickly or rolled his eyes without noticing. This was news to Arjun—it had never been mentioned in performance reviews and certainly not something he saw in himself. It stung, but it was also a gift: a blind spot had been revealed. With this new awareness, Arjun could work on it, but it raised a sobering question: *What else do I not see about myself?* Blind spots are aspects of our behavior or style apparent to others but invisible to us. They are the spinach in our teeth of leadership—everyone notices except us. And like spinach, they're not fatal, but they can undermine our effectiveness and credibility if not addressed. Many blind spots have roots in habits or traits developed long ago (often connected to the childhood influences we've been mapping).

Perhaps we act a certain way thinking it's normal, because it was normal in our family, not realizing it doesn't play well with others. Or maybe it's a defense mechanism we're oblivious to (like using humor to deflect criticism, not realizing it shuts down serious dialogue).

In this chapter, we will use a few tools to uncover blind spots: the Johari Window model for conceptualizing self-awareness, direct feedback techniques to gather others' perceptions, and reflective exercises to infer blind spots from your timeline/narrative work. It takes humility and courage to face blind spots, but doing so massively accelerates personal growth. A leader unaware of their blind spots is like a driver with blindfolds—accidents waiting to happen. A leader who uncovers and manages blind spots becomes more authentic and gains trust, because they address the issues that everyone else can see, signaling openness and a lack of ego defensiveness.

The Johari Window – Opening Up the Blind Quadrant: The Johari Window is a classic framework developed by psychologists Joseph Luft and Harrington Ingham. Imagine a four-pane window representing the interplay between what is known/not known to you and known/not known to others:

	Known to Self	Not Known to Self
Known to Others	OPEN	BLIND SPOT
Not Known to Others	HIDDEN	UNKNOWN

Figure: Johari Window – A simple 2x2 matrix. The columns are "Known to Self" vs "Not Known to Self," and the rows are "Known to Others" vs "Not Known to Others." The four cells are: Open Area (known to self and others),

Blind Spot (not known to self but known to others), Hidden/Facade (known to self but not to others), and Unknown (not known to self nor others). Our focus here is the Blind Spot area – behaviors or traits that you don't see in yourself but others do. The goal of feedback and self-discovery is to shrink the Blind Spot by moving things into the Open Area.

In leadership development, we try to enlarge the Open Area (arena of mutual understanding) by decreasing the Blind Spot (through feedback from others) and decreasing the Hidden area (through self- disclosure and authenticity). In Part I, you worked on the hidden/internal stuff through introspection. Now it's about the blind stuff—what you don't realize yet.

Blind spots can be positive or negative traits. Yes, you might be blind to a strength! For example, maybe you inspire people more than you think but you downplay it. However, typically when we say "blind spot" we mean the negatives or pitfalls we're unaware of. Common leadership blind spots include things like:

- Overestimating your listening skills (you think you're a great listener, but others find you often interrupt or dismiss ideas – as in Arjun's case).
- Underestimating the impact of your mood (you believe you hide stress well, but the team walks on eggshells because they can tell when you're in a bad mood even if you don't realize you show it).
- Believing you're empowering when you're actually micromanaging (you might think you're "helping" or being detail-oriented, but team sees it as lack of trust).
- Thinking you're decisive and clear, while others experience you as brusque or unwilling to consider input (there's a fine line between decisiveness and bulldozing; blind spots often lurk on that line).
- Assuming your value of "hard work" is evident, but others observe you don't delegate and thus you overburden yourself and sometimes slow the team (you see dedication; they see control issues or lack of trust).

- A very personal blind spot might be a prejudice or bias – e.g., you pride yourself on being fair, but others notice you tend to mentor male employees more closely than female ones, or vice versa. These can be hard to swallow but incredibly important to address.

How to find these? Ask and observe.

Inviting Feedback – The Courage to Ask "How do I come across?" By now, you may have collected some feedback informally while working on Chapter 5. Chapter 6 calls for a more structured approach. Consider doing a mini-360: reach out to a handful of people (a mix of peers, direct reports if you have, a boss or ex- boss, maybe even a client or partner) and ask for candid input on your leadership behaviors. You can frame it like, *"I'm doing a self-development exercise and I'd really value your honest perspective on a few things I might not be aware of about my leadership style. Particularly, are there any ways I hinder the team or any habits I have that could be limiting? And also, what should I do more of?"* It helps to ask for positives too (that's not just ego- soothing; knowing what to double down on is useful). By signalling you truly want constructive criticism, people are more likely to provide it.

Be ready: you might hear something surprising or even initially hard to accept. The key is to not react defensively. If someone says, "In meetings, you often cut people off," resist the urge to say "Oh that's because our meetings are short on time" etc. Just note it and say thank you. If clarity is needed, ask for an example: "Can you recall a situation where I did that? It would help me to remember." Examples bring blind spots into focus – a vague "sometimes you're dismissive" solidifies when they say "Remember last month's planning meeting, you said 'That idea will never work' to Sam without explanation and moved on – I saw his face fall." Ah, concrete scenario – now you can't unsee that. It moves from unknown to known.

You might worry that asking will make you look vulnerable or unaware. On the contrary, most people respect a leader more for seeking feedback. It shows confidence and commitment to improvement. As leadership expert Marshall Goldsmith says, successful people are great at getting feedback because they value growth over ego. So take the initiative. If direct asking feels awkward, you could use an anonymous survey (there are tools like Google Forms or SurveyMonkey, or formal 360 instruments). But often a personal approach gets richer data and allows follow-up questions.

Patterns in Feedback: Once you gather feedback, look for themes. If one person says you interrupt, it could be situational; if three people say it, it's a pattern. Compare it with your self-perception. Maybe you *knew* you tend to cut people off when excited, but you didn't realize it bothered them that much. Or you truly never realized it – boom, blind spot identified. Also pay attention to feedback that contradicts your self- image. For instance, you think you're approachable, but feedback indicates people find you intimidating. That's a classic blind spot: intention vs perception gap. Explore why: Could be your body language (maybe you frown when thinking, which they interpret as anger), or your communication style (perhaps you're terse in emails in a way you don't intend to be). This is where childhood or cultural norms may play a role: if you grew up in a family or culture where bluntness is normal, you might not realize others from different backgrounds find it harsh. One leader from a very direct Eastern European family learned that colleagues found her blunt feedback style abrasive – a shock to her, since in her upbringing it was mild compared to dinner table debates! She had to adjust by softening delivery without sacrificing honesty.

Using Assessments and Models: Another way to illuminate blind spots is through formal assessments or models like DISC, MBTI, Enneagram, etc. These are not gospel, but they can point out tendencies.

For example, a DISC profile might label you as a high-D (dominant) type – reading the description (impatient, results-focused, can steamroll others, dislikes details) might make you go "ouch, a bit true." Or MBTI might say you're an INTJ – great at strategy, sometimes not attuned to feelings – and you realize, yes, you often miss team emotional cues (blind spot!). Psychometric tools basically speed up self-awareness by giving you vocabulary and outside perspective on your behavior patterns. If you have access to any, consider using them and reflecting on the results relative to others' feedback. They may confirm what you heard, or add nuance.

One common leadership blind spot is overestimating one's communication clarity. You think you've been crystal clear in your vision or instructions, but somehow people seem confused or not aligned. This often comes out in feedback indirectly ("So what exactly are we trying to achieve?" or "I wasn't sure what you wanted on that task"). The blind spot might be that you assume everyone's on the same page because *you* see the picture in your head. The root could be impatience (maybe grown from being around slow decision- makers in youth, you rebel by being fast and assuming others catch up) or simply lack of practice in articulating thoughts. Remedy: slow down, ask others to paraphrase what you said, etc. Getting that kind of feedback ("we need more info from you about priorities") is gold – it's fixable and yields huge improvements.

Johari Window Exercise with a Team: If you manage a team, you can do a group Johari exercise, which can be very enlightening (and trust-building). The classic Johari exercise involves a list of adjectives – people pick traits they see in themselves and others pick traits they see in that person. The overlaps are Open, mismatches can reveal hidden or blind traits. For example, you might not label yourself "assertive" but others do (blind positive), or you think you're "supportive" but no one else picked that (possible blind negative or at least a disconnect). You can find Johari adjective lists online if you want to try this with willing colleagues. It can be a bit touchy-feely for some workplaces, so gauge appropriateness. Alternatively, a simpler feedback circle where each person shares one strength and one "thing to work on" for each other person can surface blind spots (with established team trust). As a leader, demonstrating openness in such a forum ("I never realized that, thank you for telling me") sets a powerful example. It signals psychological safety – that you can handle the truth, so others can too.

Connect Blind Spots to Origins: For deeper insight, try to trace any blind spot you uncover back to your timeline or childhood analysis. Often there's a connection. Say your blind spot is that you don't give praise (team says they feel unappreciated, you had no idea because you *do* appreciate them in your head). Looking back, perhaps in your family, praise was rare – maybe parents believed too much praise spoils kids, so you grew up not expecting or giving compliments. It simply didn't occur to you that people need explicit appreciation because *you* never got it and learned to do without. Recognizing that link can motivate you to change (you realize you might be perpetuating a cycle you actually resented!). Or a blind spot like Arjun's – coming off dismissive – could tie to perhaps a childhood where intellectual sparring was a sport. He might have learned to roll eyes or scoff as normal debate tactics with siblings or friends; it's not meant personally, but in a different context it *feels* personal. By identifying that, he can consciously adjust those behaviors at work.

Another example: a leader had a blind spot of avoiding conflict (he would let issues fester). Feedback from peers was that he needed to tackle problems sooner. On digging, he realized he dreaded conflict because as a child, conflict in his house meant scary fights – so he'd do anything to keep peace. That awareness helped him emotionally distance present disagreements from old traumatic ones, and to practice healthier conflict resolution. He told himself, "I'm not that powerless kid; I'm an adult who can handle a tough conversation calmly." Over time, his blind spot shrank as he actively solicited feedback: "Did I address this issue promptly and well?" and coworkers noted improvement.

Addressing Blind Spots: Identifying is step one; step two is action. For each significant blind spot identified, make an improvement plan:

- Get a Coach or Peer-Partner: Someone who knows about your blind spot and can give you a nudge in real time. If you know you tend to dominate meetings, arrange a subtle signal with a colleague (like them tapping a pen) to cue you to stop and invite others. Or ask someone you trust to observe you and debrief later ("Hey, did I come across as open in that meeting? Tell me honestly."). Over time, you'll internalize the adjustments.
- Practice New Behaviors: If your blind spot is not listening, consciously implement active listening techniques (turn off phone in meetings, paraphrase what you heard, hold back from offering your view until others have spoken). If it's lack of praise, set a goal to praise at least one person per day genuinely. If it's being dismissive, practice response phrases that validate ("That's an interesting idea, tell me more" instead of "No, won't work."). Initially these might feel forced, but they retrain your habits.
- Ask for Follow-up Feedback: After some time, check back with those who gave you the input. "I've been working on being less X (or more Y). Have you noticed a change?" People will usually be pleased you cared enough to act, and they will often happily report improvement (or give additional pointers). This not only helps you gauge progress, it also demonstrates to them your commitment – which boosts your credibility and trustworthiness greatly.

A brief caution: Don't try to fix everything at once. Pick one blind spot at a time if possible. It can be overwhelming to rewire multiple behaviors simultaneously, and you want to be genuine. Also, don't swing too far. For instance, on learning you dominate conversations, you don't want to become completely silent in a misguided overcorrection. The key is balance. Perhaps in your next meeting you aim to speak last instead of first, not never.

Beyond Blind Spots – Hidden Strengths: While we focus on negatives, do remember to uncover any hidden strengths. Maybe people see you as very calm under pressure, but you never realized it's a notable strength because inside you feel anxious (you just don't show it). Knowing that others find you calm is a strength you can lean into – in a crisis you can project that calm deliberately to help the team, even if internally you have butterflies. Or if people say you're great at mediating (and you thought that was just normal behavior), recognize that as a skill. Sometimes our most natural talents are blind to us because they come easy – we assume everyone can do that. But no, those could be your unique leadership gifts. Embrace them.

In summary, by dragging blind spots into the light, you greatly expand your Open Area, the part of you that is known both to yourself and others. That open area is where authentic leadership lives – where your intentions and your impact align. Leaders who operate in that zone are trusted because there's no facade, and they are effective because they're not tripping over unseen obstacles. Yes, it's humbling to admit flaws, but humility is itself a mark of a great leader. People will give you grace for imperfections if they see you're aware and working on them; what they don't tolerate well is a leader who is oblivious or in denial about their issues.

Having now identified what's *unseen to you but seen by others*, we will next tackle something slightly different: what's *seen by you but often not by others until it shows in behavior* – your emotional triggers and inner reactions. In Chapter 7, we explore triggers and how to pre-emptively manage them. This is the other side of self-awareness: not just behaviors but internal emotional landscapes that can erupt and catch us off guard.

Often, triggers are deeply tied to childhood experiences (as we touched on in Part I and saw with the state-shifting). Chapter 7 will equip you with tools to anticipate and handle those emotionally charged moments so they don't turn into regrettable leadership moments.

As we transition, take a moment to appreciate the work you've done so far: you've mapped your story, got real about blind spots, and you're still here! Many leaders shy away from this introspection, but you are pushing forward. Every uncomfortable revelation is one less blind spot controlling you. As the saying goes, "Better the devil you know than the devil you don't." Now you know, and knowing is liberating. The mirror can be harsh under bright lights, but it also shows you exactly where to focus your improvement efforts – and shows you the unique positive qualities you might have overlooked. Facing the mirror with honesty is an act of bravery that pays off in clarity, growth, and respect.

Let's proceed to dig into those emotional triggers and responses, to round out the excavation of your inner dynamics before we move on to building new patterns in Part III.

CHAPTER 7

TRIGGERS AND TRIPWIRES – MAPPING YOUR EMOTIONAL HOT BUTTONS

The boardroom was tense as the product review meeting went south. Elena, the product lead, was fielding tough questions about a recent failure. Outwardly she maintained a cool demeanor, but inside she felt a familiar heat rising. Then one director's comment hit a nerve: "What on earth made you think that approach would work? It's common sense it wouldn't." The phrasing, the tone – suddenly Elena was no longer a confident professional but a scolded teenager being berated by a high school teacher in front of the class. Her heart pounded, face flushed. "Excuse me?" she snapped back, voice strained. "With all due respect, it's easy to criticize in hindsight." The tension spiked. Later, Elena wondered, *Why did I react so strongly?* It was as if that comment pulled a trigger hidden deep within her, unleashing an out-of-character defensiveness. She realized that moment had roots beyond the meeting itself; it tapped into an old wound of being unfairly belittled in public.

This scenario illustrates a trigger – an emotional hot button that, when pushed, produces a reaction disproportionate to the present situation. In leadership, triggers can lead to regrettable outbursts, shutdowns, or anxiety that undermines your effectiveness. They are often the child in you reacting, rather than the adult. Many triggers were formed in formative years: some unresolved hurt, fear, or anger that lies dormant until a situation eerily resembles that original scenario (in tone, power dynamic, content, etc.). Recognizing your triggers is crucial. It's like identifying landmines in a field so you can navigate safely or defuse them.

In this chapter, we will chart your personal emotional trigger points and develop a Trigger Response Plan – strategies to respond rather than react when they're activated. By understanding what sets you off and why, you can build techniques to manage those surges. This not only prevents damage (like Elena straining relationships with the board through defensiveness), but also allows you to lead with greater composure under fire – a hallmark of mature leadership.

Identifying Your Triggers: Start by reflecting on recent incidents where you "lost it" or felt a strong emotional surge at work. "Losing it" doesn't always mean yelling; it could mean shutting down, or suddenly feeling very panicky or hurt. Use these questions:

- When was the last time I felt angry or irritated at work out of proportion to the situation? What exactly was said or done, and by whom?
- When did I feel deeply hurt or offended by something minor or unintended?
- When did I feel afraid or anxious beyond the reasonable level of risk present? (E.g., panic before a routine presentation).
- Are there recurring patterns – certain people or situations that consistently trigger me? Perhaps whenever someone challenges your expertise, or when someone raises their voice, or when facing tight deadlines with unclear instructions.

Write a list of these instances and see what common themes emerge. Elena's case, for example, might highlight "being spoken to in a condescending tone in public" as a trigger. Another leader might find "when someone questions my integrity" triggers them because maybe in childhood they were often unjustly accused by a strict parent. Someone else might be triggered by "last-minute changes" – perhaps because unpredictability as a child meant chaos or disappointment, so now any sudden change sets off alarm bells.

Now, for each trigger, trace it backwards. Ask: *What does this remind me of? When have I felt like this before?* Don't force a connection, but often something will surface. Ravi, for instance, realized that when team members procrastinated, it *infuriated* him more than was logical. On reflection, he linked it to his own childhood health struggles – he hated feeling held back or idle (since he'd been physically restricted when ill), so now any delay by others triggered frustration. Recognizing that helped him approach such situations more empathetically (he communicated why urgency mattered to him rather than just seething).

Psychologists Gass and Ansara, in the "Managing Your Triggers Toolkit," note that *triggers are wired into our upbringing and life history* . We often don't have a choice about being triggered – it's an automatic emotional hijack – but we have a choice in what we do next . The first choice is to Name it . By naming your triggers ("I'm feeling dismissed" or "I'm feeling trapped" or "I'm feeling out of control"), you bring the feeling from the subconscious to the conscious. Elena might say internally, "I'm triggered – I feel like I'm being humiliated." That act of acknowledgement engages the rational brain just enough to start intervening .

The 4-Step Trigger Plan: As introduced earlier in the context of state-shifting , a simple and effective tool for what to do when triggered is:

Name it – Literally say to yourself (even out loud, if appropriate): "I am triggered." Identify the emotion: "I'm angry" or "I'm scared" or "I'm hurt." Until you do this, your amygdala (the brain's alarm center) is in charge, and it's "helpless" . Once you name it, your prefrontal cortex (thinking brain) kicks in just a bit . It's like an adult coming into the room where a child is throwing a tantrum – the situation is still hot, but there's now someone to impose some order.

- In practice: Elena, hearing the director's scolding, could think, "Okay, I'm feeling attacked. This is triggering me big time." That split-second recognition might stop her from immediately snapping, creating a brief pause.

Take space appropriately – Remove yourself from the immediate trigger if you can do so *gracefully*. This might mean a short break, or even a deep breath if you can't physically leave. The key is "Do not act while in the triggered state". Taking space could be as simple as a sip of water to compose yourself. If the context allows, you might say, "Let's take a 5-minute break" or "I'd like to give that question some thought and come back to you." However, "appropriately" is key – storming out or abruptly going silent can inflame things more. An example of unskillful taking space: angrily saying "You're a jerk, I'm done with this" and leaving – that's venting, not constructive. ceep breaths).

- In Elena's case, since it was a formal meeting, she might not have been able to call a break. But she could pause, breathe, perhaps ask a clarifying question ("Are you suggesting the approach was obviously flawed from the start?"). That question buys time and might also put some onus back on the critic to be more constructive. Meanwhile, she's calming her physiological response.

Shift your state – This means actively doing something to change the intense emotional energy. Different techniques work for different people: deep breathing, counting to ten, reminding yourself of context ("This is my boss, not my dad – I am an adult in control here"), or even physical actions like unclenching fists, relaxing face muscles (we carry trigger tension in our body). Some find it helpful to recall a grounding truth or a mantra (e.g., "I am safe, this is not the past" or "Focus on the issue, not the insult"). The goal is to move from the emotional "child" state (hurt, scared, enraged) to the adult state (more balanced). Visualization can help too: maybe visualize that you're stepping out of your child self into your current grown self, or imagine the trigger as a fire you're cooling with water.

- One interesting approach: if possible, change the environment momentarily. For example, if a 1-1 meeting in your office gets heated, suggest moving to a different room or taking a short walk. The literal shift often helps break the emotional pattern. If you can't leave, even shifting your posture – sit up, both feet on the ground – can change your mindset.
- Elena could silently repeat to herself: "I'm not a helpless teenager, I'm a competent leader. This person's tone triggers me but I can handle it calmly." That self-talk is shifting internal state from powerless to empowered.

Deal with the situation – Now, with a cooler head, you address whatever sparked the trigger as your rational leader self. Maybe it's answering the tough question without defensiveness, or providing a counterpoint firmly but professionally, or even postponing the discussion to a better time. The idea is that once you're in a more controlled state, you respond in line with your values and goals, not from a place of emotional hijack. As Lao Tzu was quoted: *"Do you have the patience to wait till your mud settles and the water is clear?"*. Step 4 is acting once the water is clearer.

- For Elena, that would mean responding to the critical comment perhaps like: "It may seem obvious in hindsight. Here's what we saw at the time and why we made that choice. It didn't work out, but we've learned X from it." No sarcasm, no raised voice – just a clear answer. Or, if she felt too triggered to trust herself, maybe: "I hear your criticism. This is something I'd like to reflect on and give a thorough explanation for – can I send a follow-up report?" The key is she doesn't lash out or retreat permanently; she addresses it when ready.

Practicing these steps repeatedly trains you to handle triggers better. At first, you might only catch yourself *after* an outburst – that's okay, reflect and mentally rehearse how step 1-4 could have gone, so next time you catch it *earlier*. Over time, you might notice triggers sooner (perhaps heart rate spikes or face flush is your cue, or a specific thought pattern like "This is unfair!" is your clue you're triggered).

Trigger Tracker Worksheet: In Chapter 7 (source content from earlier search) we saw mention of a "Trigger Tracker Worksheet" . You might create your own. Make a table with columns: *Triggering event / My reaction / Intensity (1-10) / Coping strategy used / Outcome*. Each time you get triggered, jot it down. For example:

- Event: "Client emailed criticism late at night." Reaction: "Anxiety, couldn't sleep, drafted an angry reply (didn't send)." Intensity: "7/10." Coping: "Talked to spouse to vent, waited till morning." Outcome: "Next day felt calmer, replied diplomatically."

Logging these helps you notice patterns (maybe late-night messages trigger you more – so maybe you institute a rule of not reading work email after 9pm to protect yourself). It also celebrates progress: maybe a month later, similar event intensity feels like 4/10 and you handle it smoothly.

The Medium article noted: "Knowing what they are... we can't manage or plan for things we don't know about" . Your triggers list becomes something you *can* plan for. If you know performance reviews trigger your anxiety (reminds you of being judged by parents/teachers), you can preemptively do extra self-care around that time, or role-play the review with a friend to reduce fear. If a certain colleague triggers you by being pushy (maybe reminds you of a sibling who overshadowed you), you can plan to set boundaries early in interactions with them (tell yourself, "If John interrupts me again, I'll calmly say, 'Let me finish my point, please,' rather than swallowing resentment").

Teaching Your Team to Understand Triggers: A bonus: as you manage your triggers, you can also foster a team culture where people are aware of their triggers and support each other. Share a bit of your learning (appropriately). For example, Elena might tell her team in a debrief, "I realized I got defensive in that meeting because I felt my work was being invalidated. If you ever feel me getting defensive, you have permission to gently signal that to me – I'm working on it." That level of openness can encourage team members to share their own triggers, increasing mutual understanding. Perhaps a direct report might then feel safe to say, "I tend to shut down if someone raises their voice; it reminds me of negative past experiences, so I really appreciate calm tones even in urgency." Knowing that, Elena could adjust her style under pressure to not accidentally trigger her team member. This way, the whole team builds emotional intelligence and trust.

Keep in mind privacy and boundaries – not everyone will want to share deep histories, and that's fine. But even abstractly, a conversation about triggers (e.g., "We all have hot buttons. Let's discuss how to best communicate under stress") can yield tips like "In tense moments, I prefer direct feedback," or "I respond better if you don't email me about issues at 11pm," etc. The concept of triggers, even without delving into childhood, is a practical one for team operations.

From Triggers to Traits: There's overlap between triggers and blind spots – sometimes a blind spot is *not* realizing something triggers you. For instance, one might not see they become passive-aggressive when triggered by feeling excluded. Colleagues see the passive-aggression (blind spot behavior), and it stems from a trigger (feeling left out, rooted in past perhaps). By addressing the trigger (maybe by voicing feelings or reminding themselves it's not personal), they can eliminate the blind spot behavior. It's all interconnected.

A powerful example of mastering triggers comes from leaders who've done serious inner work. Take someone with a trauma history (say, Vasuta's mention of team challenges around gender biases). If she had been triggered by sexist behavior due to past experiences, she channeled it constructively by advising and empowering her team instead of reacting in anger. She recognized triggers (e.g., seeing women on her team doubting themselves might trigger her protective instincts) and responded by coaching them to make clear choices and stand firm . That's turning a trigger into leadership fuel – a really advanced move.

By now, you have identified personal patterns (Chapter 5), blind spots (Chapter 6), and triggers (Chapter 7). The excavation part of this journey essentially uncovers what lies beneath your leadership habits. Some findings may have been unsurprising; others might be revelations that explain so much of what you felt was mysterious about your reactions or repeated challenges.

With this deep self-awareness in hand, you are ready to transition to Part III: Transformation. That is where we take these insights and actively change our leadership behaviors and mindset – rewriting narratives, building emotional intelligence further, strengthening trust, and embedding practices that ensure continued growth. Think of Part II's work as digging up the raw ore. In Part III, we will refine it and forge new tools out of it to become the best leader you can be, not in spite of your childhood influences, but *because* of a rich understanding of them.

Before we move on, give yourself credit. Many leaders never go this deep. They plateau because unseen issues hold them back. You're doing the hard work to break through to a new level of leadership effectiveness and authenticity. As we proceed to transformation, keep your notes handy – we'll be building directly on them.

One last tip: triggers don't disappear overnight. Even with all this knowledge, you'll still get triggered (we're human). The goal is incremental improvement: from reacting badly 10 times a month to maybe 5 times, then 2, etc., and recovering faster. Celebrate those wins. Each trigger handled with grace that you couldn't manage before is tangible progress.

Now, let's turn the page to Part III and focus on transformation – applying these self-discoveries to become a more emotionally intelligent, secure, and inspiring leader than ever before.

PART III

TRANSFORMATION

Growth does not happen at the surface—it begins when awareness turns into intention. In this part, we focus on consciously evolving leadership by translating self-awareness into action: rewriting limiting narratives, strengthening emotional intelligence and resilience, and building trust and psychological safety within teams. These chapters bridge knowing and becoming, helping you integrate insight into everyday leadership so you can step into the leader you are capable of becoming—while still honoring the child you once were.

CHAPTER 9

REWRITING YOUR LEADERSHIP STORY – TURNING INSIGHT INTO VISION

Opening Story: A CEO's Awakening in São Paulo

Eduardo stood at the floor-to-ceiling windows of his São Paulo office, watching the city lights shimmer in the dusk. By all external measures, Eduardo was a successful CEO – his tech company had grown from a scrappy startup to a regional powerhouse. Yet lately, a subtle restlessness had taken hold of him. That evening, after a long board meeting, Eduardo felt the weight of his decisions differently. The discussion had turned to laying off a portion of the workforce to cut costs. The numbers made sense on paper, but something in Eduardo's conscience stirred uncomfortably as faces of loyal employees flashed through his mind.

As traffic buzzed below, Eduardo recalled a memory from his childhood. Growing up in a modest neighborhood of São Paulo, he remembered the day his father lost his job when the factory he worked at closed with no warning. The confusion and fear in his father's eyes – a proud man suddenly feeling small – left an imprint on young Eduardo. In that moment by the window, Eduardo realized the story he had been living: he'd spent years leading with an almost frantic drive for growth, partly out of fear of failure and the insecurity of not wanting to repeat his father's fate. His "success story" was still being authored by that anxious child inside who vowed to never feel helpless again.

The next morning, Eduardo made an uncharacteristic decision. He invited one of the company's long-time employees, Marcia, for coffee. Marcia's division was underperforming and likely to be cut – something the board saw as a simple financial fix. Instead of a terse meeting about targets, Eduardo asked Marcia about her goals, the challenges her team faced, and what *she* thought could turn things around. Surprised by his openness, Marcia shared candidly. She admitted that constant cost-cutting pressures had left her team demoralized and afraid to innovate. Eduardo listened, recognizing a familiar fear in her voice – the same fear of not feeling safe or valued that he knew from childhood.

That conversation in a quiet café became Eduardo's awakening. He saw that if he continued leading purely by the old script – the hard-driving executive always in control – he would fulfill a vision that wasn't truly his own, but rather a reaction to childhood insecurity. Instead, he began to imagine a new vision: a company that balanced performance with people, where employees felt secure and inspired to give their best. In the weeks that followed, Eduardo proposed a bold pivot to the board. Rather than immediate layoffs, they would launch a "Moonshot Lab" initiative inviting teams to propose innovative cost-saving projects. He painted a vision of an organization where everyone, from interns to executives, felt ownership of its future – a future in which the company thrived *because* it cared for its people's growth.Some board members were skeptical. But Eduardo's conviction was contagious; it was grounded in personal insight and genuine passion. He shared the story of his father with the board for the first time, explaining why building a resilient, loyal workforce was personal to him. In doing so, he transformed the conversation from spreadsheets to vision. Over the next quarter, Marcia's team – rejuvenated by the trust placed in them – identified a process improvement that saved significant costs without layoffs. The "Moonshot Lab" idea generated multiple innovations, and Eduardo's company emerged more profitable *and* more united. Eduardo had rewritten his leadership story, turning hard-won insight into a guiding vision for his company's next chapter.

The Stories We Tell Ourselves as Leaders

Every leader carries an invisible book of stories – narratives about who we are, how we should lead, and what our past means. These internal stories often trace back to experiences in our formative years. In Eduardo's case, a childhood memory of his father's job loss quietly shaped his leadership decisions decades later. We are all storytellers, and the most influential stories are the ones we tell ourselves about ourselves. By mid-career, many leaders have an internalized narrative: perhaps "I must be tough to be respected," or "I always have to prove I'm good enough," or "If I don't control every detail, everything will fall apart." Such narratives can become self-fulfilling prophecies that limit our leadership potential.

Psychologists call this our "narrative identity," the internalized story that gives our life coherence and meaning. Crucially, this narrative is not fixed – it can be examined and rewritten. As leadership expert Bill George observes, *"authentic leaders consistently say they find their motivation through understanding their own stories."* In other words, looking inward at the origins of your leadership approach can unlock powerful motivation. Perhaps you lead with empathy because you remember feeling unheard as a child, or you chase ambitious goals because you learned to crave validation through achievement. These insights, once brought to light, allow you to decide which parts of your story to carry forward and which to rewrite.

Recognizing Your Current Script: Start by reflecting on what *story* might subconsciously be guiding your leadership. Ask yourself:

- *What early experience or influential figure might have planted the script I'm following?* (For example, did a childhood of scarce resources make you extremely risk-averse, or did a mentor's confidence in you ignite a lifelong drive?)
- *When I face a crisis or big decision, what inner voice or memory tends to surface?* (Is it a cautious parent urging safety, or perhaps a competitive coach pushing you to "win at all costs"?)
- *What labels or narratives have I internalized about myself?* (Perhaps "I'm the underdog who must fight for everything" or "I'm the caretaker who must please everyone.")

Journaling or talking these through with a coach or trusted colleague can be illuminating. You may discover, for instance, that you've been cast in the role of "the perfectionist" since youth, or that you see yourself as "the survivor" who must handle everything alone. These storylines often start as coping mechanisms in childhood or early career and then tag along, sometimes outliving their usefulness.

When Insight Dawns: Eduardo's awakening in São Paulo exemplified what can happen when a leader gains personal insight. He realized his relentless drive came from an old fear. Such moments of clarity can feel almost literary – like suddenly understanding the chapter of a book you've been unknowingly writing. These insights might come from a reflective pause, feedback from others, or even from burnout forcing you to ask *"Why am I really doing this?"* However they come, insights are the raw material for transformation. They shine a light on the gap between the story you've been living and the story you aspire to create.

One CEO of a global manufacturing firm described a similar epiphany: "I always pushed my team mercilessly on deadlines. Only after my health scare did I trace that behavior back to my childhood poverty – I was terrified of losing everything. Recognizing that freed me to lead from hope instead of fear." Such reflections underscore a powerful truth:

your past isn't a prison sentence for your leadership style. It's a source of lessons and strength, once you decide to interpret it that way.

From Insight to Vision: Using Personal Reflections to Shape Your Future

Insight alone is powerful, but insight combined with vision is transformative. Rewriting your leadership story means taking the wisdom gained from reflection and using it to paint a compelling picture of the leader you want to be and the future you want to create. It's the bridge Eduardo crossed – moving from *understanding* his old motivators to *articulating* a new leadership vision founded on his values.

What does "vision" mean in this context? It's not only about organizational goals or financial targets (though those are important); it's about a clear and inspiring picture of a better future that is personally meaningful to you as a leader. In short, it's a positive narrative about where you and your team or organization are headed, and *why it matters*. The best visions often have their roots in personal insight. Consider the story of Howard Schultz, former CEO of Starbucks. Schultz grew up in a poor family and remembered the hardship his father faced when he lost his job and medical insurance. That childhood memory fueled Schultz's vision of building a company that treats employees with dignity and provides them healthcare and support – "the kind of company where his father could work and have a chance of putting food on the table, even after an injury." His personal story became inseparable from Starbucks' corporate vision and values. In this way, a wound from the past was transformed into a purpose for the future.

By tapping into your own story, you ensure that your vision isn't just a generic statement, but a passionate commitment. People can sense the difference. When you speak from a place of personal conviction, your vision gains credibility and emotional resonance. In Eduardo's case, once he connected his strategy (innovating to save jobs) to his personal narrative (valuing security and loyalty after seeing his father lose a job), his message landed with greater impact. Team members heard not just a plan, but a *principle*. Insight gave his vision moral weight.

Crafting an Empowering Leadership Narrative: Rewriting your story doesn't mean fabricating a new past; it means reframing your understanding of the past and choosing what story will guide you forward. Here's a systematic approach to turn insight into an empowering vision:

1. Claim Your Origin Story: What key life events, challenges, or triumphs have shaped your values? Rather than seeing them as baggage, frame them as your unique leadership *origin story*. For example, "Growing up moving from city to city taught me to adapt quickly – now I use that adaptability to lead through change." Claim these experiences proudly as the bedrock of your leadership philosophy.
2. Identify the ***Turning Points***: Reflect on moments of adversity or epiphany (like Eduardo's realization in the boardroom). These turning points often carry a lesson or reveal a value. Perhaps a failure early in your career taught you humility and the value of listening. Or mentoring a struggling employee showed you the importance of empathy. These turning points are like plot twists that can redefine your narrative. Ask: *What did I learn, and how does it inform the leader I want to be?*
3. Envision the Future (Your Leadership Vision Statement): With those lessons in mind, articulate a vision for your leadership. This might take the form of a personal mission statement or a vivid description of a future state for your team/organization. Make it inspiring and anchored in your values. For instance: *"I envision building an organization where innovation and compassion coexist – where we dare to take risks, and we take care of our people along the way."* The best vision statements are specific enough to be meaningful, but broad enough to

be aspirational. They connect the personal ("compassion" born of your life lesson) with the universal ("innovation" driving the business).

4. Test for Authenticity: A rewritten story must ring true. When you articulate your new narrative or vision, it should *feel* authentic and energizing to you. If it doesn't, keep refining. Sometimes fear or old habits may cause us to water down a bold vision. Revisit Step 1 and 2 if needed, to ensure you're truly incorporating your deepest insights. One authenticity check: share your leadership vision informally with a close colleague or mentor who knows you well. If they respond with "*That sounds just like you,*" you're on the right track. If they look puzzled, you might be reciting what you *think* a leader's vision should sound like, rather than speaking from your gut.
5. Align Actions with the New Narrative: This is crucial – a story is only as powerful as the actions it inspires. Consider what behaviors, decisions, or habits need to change for your new narrative to come to life. If your old story was "I can't show weakness," and your new narrative values vulnerability and trust-building, then perhaps a concrete action is to start admitting when you need help or when you make a mistake. If your vision statement centers on inclusivity, ensure you are regularly inviting input from quieter team members. Essentially, walk the talk of your new story. This alignment builds credibility with others and reinforces the narrative for yourself. *(We'll explore team trust and empathy more in Chapter 11 – building on the idea that a secure leader openly aligns actions with values.)*

By following these steps, you effectively perform a narrative "reset." You're not erasing your past – you're reinterpreting it in a way that serves your growth. It's akin to the literary technique of a hero's journey: the hero (you) returns from a period of trials (your insights gained from challenges) with a *gift* – a new understanding and vision – that will benefit the community (your team or organization).

Leadership Framework: From Personal Story to Shared Vision

Turning personal insight into a leadership vision also has a cascading effect: it shapes how you communicate and rally others. Great leaders are often great storytellers. Once you have clarity on your own narrative and vision, share it. Marshall Ganz, a Harvard leadership lecturer, speaks about "public narrative" – the story of self, the story of us, and the story of now. In practical terms, this means:

- Story of Self: Why I lead (your origin and values).
- Story of Us: What *we* stand for together (shared values and mission).
- Story of Now: What challenge or opportunity we face, and why we must act.

By weaving your personal story into a collective vision, you invite others to see themselves in the narrative. Eduardo did this when he told the board and employees *why* protecting jobs mattered to him personally and connected it to the company's future success – he turned his private insight into a public rallying cry.

Consider using storytelling techniques in your next all-hands meeting or strategy presentation. Instead of diving straight into KPIs, start with a personal anecdote that led you to champion this strategy. You might say: *"When I was a new manager, I made the mistake of hoarding information – and I nearly sunk a project because my team felt in the dark. That lesson stayed with me. It's why our new vision emphasizes transparency at every level, and why I'm committed to open communication."* Such an opener not only humanizes you, it grounds the vision in real experience. It demonstrates that the vision isn't coming from a consultant's playbook – it's born of hard-earned wisdom.

Leadership Narrative Checklist: To ensure you're leveraging your story effectively, ask yourself the following:

- Have I articulated my leadership values clearly, and are they linked to real experiences? (E.g., "Integrity matters to me because years ago I dealt with a dishonest boss who nearly derailed my career, and I promised myself I'd do differently.")
- Does my team know ***why*** I care about the things I emphasize? If not, find opportunities to briefly explain the origin. People will commit more to a vision when they understand the leader's genuine motivation.
- Am I using my insight to inspire, not to impose? Rewriting your story is personal, but its purpose is to propel everyone forward. Ensure that sharing your narrative is in service of building a shared vision, not just self-disclosure. The goal is collective inspiration – your story is a bridge, not a pedestal.

Finally, remember that rewriting your leadership story is not a one-time event. Just as companies periodically revisit their strategic vision, leaders should revisit their personal vision too. As you continue to grow, new insights will emerge – and you may refine your narrative further. *Transformation is an ongoing process.* By continually choosing to respond to challenges with wisdom drawn from your story (rather than reacting from old wounds or knee-jerk habits), you model to everyone that growth is a lifelong journey.

Eduardo's story in São Paulo had a happy evolution: his personal awakening led to a powerful vision that not only averted layoffs but sparked innovation and loyalty. The real victory, however, was internal – he freed himself from an outdated narrative of fear and stepped into a new story of leadership defined by vision and values. In the next chapters, we will build on this foundation: once you have rewritten your leadership story for yourself, how do you heal the remaining old wounds that could sabotage your vision, build secure relationships of trust that allow your vision to flourish with your team, and remain resilient under pressure as you live out your new narrative? Each element is key to sustaining the transformation that rewriting your story begins.

Transitioning now from the realm of personal insight and vision, we turn to the deeper emotional work of leadership transformation. The next chapter delves into how to heal the hidden *inner child* wounds that often lurk beneath the surface of our leadership behaviors – and how doing so can empower you to lead with confidence and compassion rather than fear.

CHAPTER 10

HEALING OLD WOUNDS – FROM INNER CHILD TO EMPOWERED LEADER

Opening Story: The Perfectionist from Pune

Aarav's hands trembled slightly as he straightened a stack of project reports on his desk for the third time that morning. It was 7:00 AM in Pune, and the office was still quiet. As the regional director for a fast- growing pharmaceutical startup, Aarav had built a reputation for perfectionism. Under his leadership, nothing left the department unless he had scrutinized every detail. His relentless standards had produced excellent quality control – but it had also created bottlenecks and frayed nerves among his team.

This particular morning, Aarav was preparing for a quarterly review presentation to the company's CEO. He had spent the entire night refining his slides and double-checking data. Now, utterly exhausted, he noticed a small typo on slide 27 – and felt panic welling up as if the entire project's credibility hung on that one mistake. As he hurriedly fixed the error, his mind raced back in time to a memory from primary school: he was 10 years old, proudly bringing home a math test score of 95%. Instead of praise, his father's face fell into a frown. "What happened to the other 5%?" his father asked flatly. Aarav remembered the sting of that moment. It was the first time he felt that *almost perfect* was essentially a failure.

Decades later, that childhood wound still drove him. Aarav's pursuit of perfection was, in truth, an attempt to avoid the shame and disappointment of that "missing 5%." Yet, as he sat in the empty office, he felt another pang – a realization that his team had begun walking on eggshells around him. They were afraid to take risks or share half-formed ideas, knowing he might seize on any imperfection. In their eyes, he often saw the same nervousness he once felt with his father. The thought hit him hard: *Had he become the very figure of impossible expectations that he himself had feared as a child?*

Later that day, the CEO review did not go as expected. Despite Aarav's immaculate slides, the CEO seemed concerned. "Our innovation pipeline has slowed down," she noted. "I see great execution on current projects, but fewer new ideas in the last quarter. What's going on in your division?" Aarav started to respond with stock phrases – blaming regulatory hurdles, market conditions – but stopped himself. He realized those were excuses. Taking a breath, he spoke honestly: "I think I might be part of the problem. I've been running things so tightly that my team is afraid to experiment or speak up. We're executing, but not innovating – and that's on me." It was a bold admission, and as the words left his mouth, Aarav felt a weight lifting.

That evening, instead of burying himself in more work, Aarav did something he hadn't done in years. He drove to a quiet temple on the outskirts of Pune that he used to visit with his grandfather as a boy. Sitting on the cool marble floor, he reflected on how his perfectionism, once a source of pride, had become a double-edged sword. He thought about the shy smiles of relief on his team members' faces earlier when he returned from the CEO meeting and *for once* thanked them for their hard work without adding a "but next time, do better." It was a small change in behavior, but it felt significant.

Over the next few weeks, Aarav took deliberate steps to heal the old wound that had long driven him. He initiated "idea afternoons" where the team would brainstorm with no critique allowed – a radical change from his previous approach. He confessed in one meeting, "I realize I've been obsessing over getting everything 100% right. But innovation is messy. I had to remind myself that 90% success with 10% learned from failure can be more valuable than 100% safe ideas." The team was stunned – was this the same boss who once berated an engineer for a minor calculation error? In sharing his vulnerability, Aarav noticed his team's demeanor shift. They grew more open, more willing to take ownership. One young scientist even said, "It's inspiring to see that you trust us to learn from mistakes, sir."

The real transformation, however, was inside Aarav. Each time he resisted the urge to micromanage or criticize, it felt like a small healing of that 10-year-old boy who had felt "not enough." He started to appreciate his own progress and his team's efforts rather than fixate on flaws. Where earlier stress and self- doubt often kept him awake, he now slept better, content that he was doing his best and allowing others to do the same. The perfectionist from Pune was slowly, surely, becoming an empowered leader – one who leads from confidence and trust rather than insecurity and fear.

Understanding the "Inner Child" in Leadership

Aarav's story might sound familiar in its themes, if not its specifics. Many of us in leadership have some version of that childhood moment – an event or environment in our early years that left emotional imprints. Those early imprints form the psyche of our "inner child," a concept psychologists use to describe the childlike part of our subconscious that holds onto experiences, emotions, and learned behaviors from youth. When that inner child's needs are unmet or wounds unhealed, it doesn't stay quietly in the past – it shows up in adult life, including at work, often in surprising ways.

The Inner Child at the Office? It might feel odd to think that the boardroom could be influenced by the playground, but consider how unresolved childhood experiences can manifest in leadership behavior:

A leader who grew up with constant criticism might develop an overactive inner critic, second- guessing themselves and others. This can lead to indecisiveness or alternatively, overly harsh criticism of team members – essentially passing on the criticism that still echoes in their own head.

- Someone who experienced abandonment or unreliable caregivers might struggle with trust and delegation, leading them to micromanage or hold all decisions tightly (a fear-driven need for control).
- A person who felt unheard as a child might either become a leader who doesn't listen (because they never learned healthy communication) or one who overcorrects by trying too hard to please everyone (to avoid anyone feeling ignored).
- As with Aarav, an upbringing that equated love with achievement can produce a perfectionist leader – setting impossibly high standards, having a low tolerance for mistakes, and often burning out themselves and their team in pursuit of approval that can never quite be earned.

Psychologists note that an *"unhealed inner child"* often reveals itself through emotional triggers and disproportionate reactions in adults . For leaders, this might look like reacting with unusual anger to minor provocations, feeling devastated by constructive feedback, or experiencing imposter syndrome despite evident success. These reactions are clues that something deeper is at play – essentially, the inner child "running the show" at times. As one leadership coach put it, *"The boardroom table can become a sandbox when unresolved childhood emotions are triggered."*

Signs Your Inner Child Might Be Influencing Your Leadership: Do any of these ring true for you?

- Heightened emotional reactivity: You find yourself overreacting – perhaps snapping at a team member for a small mistake or feeling extreme anxiety over routine performance evaluations. This could indicate old emotions (like fear of failure or rejection) are being stirred.
- Insecurity and approval-seeking: You constantly seek validation from your boss or board, or you have a hard time making decisions without consensus because you fear criticism. An unhealed inner child often *"harbors insecurity and a constant need for approval,"* which can compromise decision- making.
- Difficulty trusting others: You struggle to delegate and often suspect others will let you down. This can stem from past betrayals or abandonment fears – and it's detrimental to team productivity and morale.
- Perfectionism and micromanagement: As we saw with Aarav, the drive to be perfect often originates from childhood attempts to earn love or avoid punishment. Leaders with this trait may set unrealistic standards, leading to burnout and a stifled team culture.
- Avoidance of conflict or confrontation: Perhaps you go to great lengths to keep peace, even when issues need addressing, because deep down conflict makes you feel unsafe (maybe your household was full of explosive conflict, or the opposite, and you never learned to handle it). Avoiding necessary conflict can foster a toxic work culture where issues fester .
- Overpersonalization: You take work setbacks *very* personally – a lost sale or a project hiccup makes you feel like a failure. This can be a sign that your self-worth got tied to external achievements early on, a common inner child wound.

If you recognize yourself in a few of these patterns, take heart – you're far from alone. In fact, many top leaders have privately admitted that their drive or style originated from childhood compensations. The difference between a reactive leader and a resilient, empowered leader often lies in who is in charge internally: the wounded child or the wise adult. Healing those old wounds shifts that balance.

One striking example comes from an Inc. magazine piece where Earvin "Magic" Johnson recounted how a childhood lesson from his father turned him into a perfectionist overnight. As a kid, Magic tried to do a half-hearted job during a freezing winter morning of work, and his father sternly corrected him, linking effort in chores to effort in life. *"I turned into a perfectionist right at that moment on that day,"* Johnson recalls.

In his basketball career, that perfectionism drove him to greatness. But in a business leadership context, Magic later had to learn to moderate that impulse – to allow his team members the latitude to make mistakes and grow. His story shows how a childhood lesson can be both a strength and a shackle; the key is to become aware of it and manage it consciously.

From Wounds to Wisdom: The Process of Healing

Healing your inner child doesn't mean dwelling in the past or blaming those who raised you. It means acknowledging that past experiences – good, bad, or ugly – influence your present, and then taking steps to address any pain or skewed beliefs left over. The ultimate goal is to lead from a place of wholeness and confidence – effectively leading as an empowered adult, rather than an anxious child. Here's how you can begin that transformation:

Recognize the Wound: You can't heal what you don't see. Aarav's first step was realizing his perfectionism was rooted in that childhood memory of not feeling good enough. This recognition often requires honest self-reflection. Pay attention to moments when your emotional response seems overly intense or not entirely rational for the situation. Those are neon arrows pointing to an underlying wound or unmet need. For instance, do you feel a surge of panic when you get critical feedback (pointing to a wound around self-worth)? Do you shut down when team members argue (pointing to a childhood pattern that conflict isn't safe)? These emotional clues are invaluable. Journaling about them or discussing with a mentor/coach can help connect present triggers to past experiences .

Give Your Inner Child a Voice: This might sound unconventional in a leadership context, but it's powerful. When you're upset or anxious, pause and ask yourself: *"What is my inner child feeling right now?"* Maybe "She's feeling scared that she will look stupid," or "He feels like he's going to be abandoned if this fails." It can be surprisingly effective to identify these vulnerable feelings. It creates a bit of distance between *you (the competent adult leader)* and the *emotion (the child part)*. This is the first step in reparenting yourself – effectively becoming the compassionate, reassuring voice that your younger self needed . For example, Aarav might tell his inner child, "It's okay, you did your best, and even if someone isn't happy, you're still worthy." This self-talk, while private, rewires the brain over time to replace knee-jerk fear responses with calmer, more rational responses.

Challenge and Reframe the Belief: Often, a childhood wound carries an implicit belief or story. "I'm only lovable if I'm perfect." "People will leave me if I disagree with them." "Expressing emotion is a weakness." Once you identify such a belief, challenge its validity as an adult. Is it really true? Usually, it's not – it was just a child's interpretation of circumstances. Now, reframe it. For instance: instead of "I must be perfect to succeed," reframe to "Striving for excellence is good, but embracing imperfection allows me and my team to learn and innovate." This reframing is akin to "telling yourself a different story" about the situation . It snuffs out the perpetual inner drama and replaces it with a narrative that serves you in the here and now. Aarav did this reframing by shifting from "If there's a flaw, I'm a failure" to "Flaws and failures are part of growth."

Practice Self-Compassion: Beating yourself up for having these struggles only keeps you in the child role. Instead, practice what psychologist Kristin Neff calls *self-compassion* – treat yourself with the same understanding and kindness you'd offer a good friend. Remind yourself that everyone has insecurities and scars; yours just happen to be manifesting in your leadership right now. When that critical voice in your head starts (often an echo of a parent or authority from your past), consciously counter it with a supportive voice. For example, if you think, "I messed up that presentation; I'm not cut out for this," catch it and respond as a mentor might: "One presentation doesn't define you. You can learn from this and be better next time." This isn't just touchy-feely advice – research shows that self-compassion boosts resilience and emotional well-being, which in turn makes you a more balanced leader. By soothing your inner child's fear or shame with empathy, you defuse its power.

Seek Connection and Support: Sometimes healing deep-seated wounds goes beyond what you can do alone. Seeking out a professional – such as a therapist or executive coach familiar with inner child or emotional development work – can be immensely helpful. There is no shame in this; in fact, it's a mark of an empowered leader to leverage resources for growth. A skilled counselor can guide you through processes like inner child work therapy, which might include visualization exercises where you mentally "visit" your younger self at a key moment and offer comfort or perspective that was missing then . It might also draw on modalities like attachment theory or cognitive reframing to help you build new patterns. The point is, you don't have to DIY all your healing.

As the saying goes, "what is not repaired is repeated." Investing time to repair through counseling or coaching can break the cycle of repetition. Many leaders privately credit therapy or coaching as a turning point that made them not just better humans, but better bosses.

In addition, build a new support system in daily life. Cultivate relationships with people who provide the kind of encouragement and stability you might have lacked earlier. In a sense, assemble a "personal board of advisors" who serve as nurturing voices – mentors, peers, even supportive family members or friends who keep you grounded. As BetterUp's career coaches often advise, *"be your own parent"* when needed , but also surround yourself with others who uplift you. This helps replace old patterns of seeking approval from the wrong places; instead, you're reinforcing your worth through healthy connections.

1. Embrace New Behaviors Gradually: As you heal internally, start taking small behavioral risks to reinforce your growth. If you normally avoid conflict, try respectfully confronting a minor issue and note that the world doesn't end – perhaps the relationship even improves. If you tend to micromanage, delegate a task that you'd typically control tightly, and let it run its course (maybe it won't be done exactly your way, but it may still turn out fine or even better). These small experiments will likely be uncomfortable, but each time you survive and succeed, your inner child gains evidence that the old fear was overstated. Over time, the new behaviors become part of your comfort zone.
   Aarav's "idea afternoons" were a great example – initially, sitting back and not interjecting when his team's ideas weren't perfectly fleshed out made him *itch* to jump in. But he bit his tongue and let it flow. To his surprise, not only did the sky not fall, but his team produced a couple of innovative approaches that he might never have heard under the old regime. That positive outcome further healed his trust – both in others and in himself to handle imperfection.

2. Acknowledge Progress and Keep Healing: The journey from inner child to empowered leader is not linear or finite. You may find that you make great strides, then an unexpected stressor triggers an old reaction. That's okay. It's in those moments that you can measure how far you've come by how differently you handle it now. Perhaps earlier Aarav would have lashed out at an employee to cover his insecurity; now he recognizes the flare of anger as a sign to pause and address his own feelings first. That's progress. Celebrate it. Healing is often two steps forward, one step back, but the general trajectory is upward if you stay committed.

And what does an empowered leader look like on the other side of this healing? It's someone who leads from a secure sense of self. Instead of being driven by unconscious fears or unmet needs, you are driven by purpose, values, and a genuine desire to serve and achieve. Challenges are no longer threats to your ego, but puzzles to solve or opportunities to grow. You can be emotionally present and empathetic with your team because you've learned to be so with yourself. In fact, leaders who have done inner work often become champions of positive culture: they create safer spaces for others because they know the pain of not having had that safety. They mentor and develop their people, in effect becoming the kind of supportive figure they themselves once needed.

A powerful real-world example is the transformation of an executive we'll call Meera, who led a non-profit in Mumbai. Early in her tenure, she struggled with intense imposter syndrome (her inner child's fear of not being "good enough" after growing up in poverty). It made her defensive and controlling. After a mentor encouraged her to work through those fears, Meera gradually embraced her story – she started sharing with her team why she was so passionate about the mission (having lived the issues firsthand) and admitted her own learning curve. This vulnerability and self-acceptance turned her into a magnetic, empowering leader. She reported that decisions got better because her team contributed more openly, and she no longer felt the crippling anxiety before board meetings that she once did. As Meera put it, *"I finally feel like the leader I was meant to be, not the scared child I used to be."*

Turning Healing into Leadership Strength

Healing old wounds is deeply personal, but in leadership it yields very public results. When you move from inner child to empowered leader, it shows up in daily interactions and big decisions alike. Here are some positive shifts you can expect:

- Increased Emotional Intelligence: You become more self-aware and better at self-regulation. Instead of reacting impulsively from emotional triggers, you respond thoughtfully. This sets a tone for your team – a leader who is calm under pressure and aware of their impact can diffuse tensions and model stability.

Empathy and Trust: Having confronted your own vulnerabilities, you're more attuned to others'. Leaders who have done inner work often listen more deeply and judge less. This creates an atmosphere of trust. Team members start to mirror that empathy with each other, improving collaboration. As one LinkedIn article noted, *"By acknowledging and addressing these unresolved issues, leaders can cultivate a more authentic and compassionate leadership style"*– exactly the kind of style that earns loyalty.

- Greater Creativity and Risk-Taking: When the fear of failure or need for approval is no longer calling the shots, innovation can flourish. You and your team feel freer to experiment because mistakes are no longer seen as catastrophic, but as learning opportunities. Paradoxically, by letting go of the obsession to never fail, you likely will fail less – because you'll take calculated risks that lead to breakthroughs (and handle any setbacks resiliently).

- Stronger Relationships and Conflict Resolution: An empowered leader doesn't fear conflict for personal reasons, so you can approach disagreements objectively and empathetically. You're more likely to *respond* rather than *react* in the face of conflict. This encourages a culture where issues are addressed before they fester. You might even find yourself coaching others in healthy conflict, turning potentially divisive moments into trust-building exercises.
- Authentic Confidence: This is not the bravado or mask that some leaders wear, but a quieter confidence that comes from knowing *"I can handle whatever comes because I've handled my own demons."* That kind of confidence is contagious. Teams perform better when their leader is confidently humble – open about what they know and don't know, secure in their ability to navigate uncertainty. It's the opposite of the brittle ego that can crumble or become tyrannical under stress.

A useful exercise is to periodically do a quick self-check-in with these points, almost like a symptoms vs. signs list. Are you seeing the signs of an empowered leader in how you behave and feel? For instance:

- When a project goes off-track, do you seek solutions with the team (empowered), or do you silently fear it will expose you as inadequate (inner child)?
- When giving feedback, do you come from a place of wanting to help others grow (empowered), or from irritation that they made you look bad (inner child)?
- When receiving feedback, can you hear it and discern useful points (empowered), or do you feel defensive and hear only personal attack (inner child)?

If you catch remnants of the latter, that's okay – it just flags areas for a bit more healing or awareness. We're all works in progress.

Leader, Heal Thyself – and Lead Forward: It's worth noting that healing isn't just about fixing problems; it's about releasing untapped potential. Many leaders discover that as they heal old wounds, they unlock strengths that were dormant. The empathy born of suffering becomes their superpower in understanding customers or motivating employees. The discipline they developed to cope with tough times becomes the backbone of their execution excellence. The key is, those strengths are now wielded by choice, not out of unconscious compulsion.

Before we leave this chapter, let's revisit Aarav briefly. In subsequent quarters, Aarav's division in Pune not only caught up in innovation, it surpassed other divisions. His team reported higher engagement scores and lower turnover. The company's CEO took notice and asked Aarav to lead a workshop for other managers on fostering a culture of learning (and yes, making peace with imperfection). Perhaps the most touching outcome: one of Aarav's direct reports, who used to suffer from anxiety under his old management style, said to him, *"I enjoy coming to work now. I feel like I can bring my whole self, not just my 'error-free' self."* That comment resonated deeply; it was evidence that in healing himself, Aarav had also created a more healing environment for others – an environment he wished *he* had earlier in his career.

In the next chapter, we will explore how an empowered leader – secure in themselves after doing this inner work – can create exactly that kind of environment for their team. We'll look at building trust and empathy in your team, turning your personal transformation into a foundation for collective success. After all, leadership is not just an inside job; it manifests in relationships. As you become a more secure leader, you are called to become a *secure base* for others. Let's examine how trust, empathy, and psychological safety become the currency of leadership once you've shed the old insecurities.

CHAPTER 11

THE SECURE LEADER – BUILDING TRUST AND EMPATHY IN YOUR TEAM

Opening Story: From Tokyo with Trust

The midday sun filtered gently through the shōji screens of the conference room in Tokyo. Akiro, the managing director of a Japanese tech firm, sat across from Daniel, an American consultant brought in to improve the company's project management processes. Weeks into the collaboration, progress was slow and tension hung in the air. Akiro's team was polite but guarded with Daniel, often deferring to their boss's opinions in meetings and offering little direct input. Daniel felt frustrated that he wasn't getting the honest feedback or creative brainstorming he expected. Meanwhile, Akiro watched with growing concern as cultural misunderstandings piled up.

In one meeting, Daniel had casually challenged one of Akiro's proposals, not realizing that in Akiro's eyes, this public questioning undermined his credibility with his team. The team members, for their part, grew wary; they retreated further into silence, not wanting to get caught in what felt like a brewing conflict between their leader and the outsider. By week four, the project was on the verge of stalling. It wasn't a matter of competence – all the individuals were skilled – it was a matter of trust. Or rather, the lack of it.

Sensing the impasse, Akiro decided to take an unconventional step. That Friday, he invited Daniel and the team leads to an informal nomikai – a traditional after-work drinks gathering, something usually reserved for internal team bonding. At a cozy izakaya down a neon-lit Shibuya alley, Akiro surprised everyone by loosening his usually formal demeanor. Halfway through the evening, he stood up, raised a toast, and said, "I have a confession. The past weeks, I have been too rigid. Daniel, in our meetings I was uncomfortable with how directly you spoke – but I realize that's exactly why we brought you in, to speak openly and shake us up. I want my team to hear that I trust you, and I trust them. Please, everyone, share what you really think. Let's build something great together."

There was a moment of stunned silence. One of Akiro's senior engineers, Mika, spoke up softly, "Director, does that mean…if we disagree or have bad news, it's okay to speak?" Akiro nodded, "Yes. I realize I haven't made it easy. I was too worried about everything appearing perfect. That changes now." Daniel, sipping his sake, felt a weight lift. In that simple, heartfelt admission, Akiro had done something powerful – he had made himself vulnerable and signaled to the team that *psychological safety* was now on the menu. It was as if the tight formal armor everyone wore had loosened a notch. Laughter became a bit more genuine as the night went on.

The following Monday, things noticeably shifted. In the project meeting, Akiro himself opened by recounting a mistake he made early in his career and how he learned from it. The team's eyes widened – their boss was *humanizing* himself. Daniel presented a contentious idea – and this time, Akiro invited Mika to voice her concerns about it. When Mika hesitated, Akiro gently encouraged, "It's alright, I really want to hear your perspective." She carefully articulated a flaw in the plan. To Daniel's surprise (and relief), Akiro thanked her for the honesty and the team set about collectively refining the idea. The meeting ended with more energy than it began. People felt heard, and Daniel finally felt he was getting authentic input.

Over the next month, what had been a stalled project turned into a high-performing collaboration. The team began to volunteer ideas proactively. Daniel adjusted his style too – he learned the value of listening first and building relationships (taking a cue from Japanese norms) before diving into critique. What bridged their cultural and communication gap was the trust that Akiro intentionally cultivated. He went out of his way to be transparent – even sharing some uncertainties about the project's direction – and invited suggestions. He made it a point to publicly acknowledge team members who took initiative or highlighted problems early (rather than, as before, silently expecting them to always defer).

By the time the project concluded successfully, Akiro's firm not only had a new project management process but a new team culture. At the celebratory dinner, Mika mentioned to Daniel, "This feels like a different team than a few months ago. I think we all grew a new level of respect. I used to be afraid of making a mistake in front of Director Akiro. Now I know he'll back me up even if things go wrong." Daniel smiled and added, "And I learned that trust isn't automatic – it's earned and given bit by bit. But once it's there, work gets a whole lot easier."

The Tokyo story illustrates a fundamental truth in leadership: *the highest-performing teams run on trust and empathy.* When Akiro shifted from a traditionally authoritative stance to a secure, empathetic one – showing vulnerability and inviting others in – he unlocked his team's potential. In this chapter, we dive into how becoming a secure leader allows you to build that trust and empathy in your team, creating an environment where people feel safe to contribute their best.

Why Trust Is the Foundation of High Performance

It's often said that "trust is the glue of a team." Modern research bears that out in concrete terms. High- trust teams are not just happier; they substantially outperform low-trust teams. Consider this striking statistic: teams with high trust levels are about 50% more productive than those with low trust .When trust is present, people spend less energy watching their backs or second-guessing colleagues, and more energy on collaborative, creative work. Trust, in essence, reduces friction – decisions get made faster, information flows freely, and everyone can focus on the task rather than office politics or self-protection.

Google's famous study on team effectiveness, *Project Aristotle*, reinforced that psychological safety – a climate of trust and mutual respect – was the number one predictor of a high-performing team . In fact, the composition of the team (who is on it) mattered far less than how team members interacted. Teams where people felt safe to speak up, take risks, and be themselves consistently outperformed those where fear or uncertainty reigned . Specifically, Google found that the best teams *"engaged with each other in a consistent practice of empathy and actively sought each member's contributions."* Empathy and inclusion weren't just nice-to-haves; they were game-changers for results.

What Trust Looks Like in Action: In a team setting, trust manifests as a set of behaviors and norms. Some signs you have a high-trust, high-empathy team include:

- Open Communication: Team members freely share ideas, including dissenting ones, without fear of ridicule or retribution. People report bad news or admit mistakes early, rather than hiding them. (In low-trust environments, there's a lot of information hoarding and sugar-coating of reality.)

Willingness to Help and Ask for Help: Members readily offer assistance and also feel comfortable asking for help when they're stuck. As one leadership insight puts it, *"Asking for help is a sign of the secure leader – one who engages everyone to reach goals."* This attitude, when modeled by the leader, spreads in the team.

Constructive Conflict: Differences of opinion are viewed as a path to better solutions, not as personal attacks. In a trusting team, debates focus on ideas, and once a decision is made, everyone commits without bitterness. (We'll revisit conflict in the next chapter on resilience, but note that trust is what makes healthy conflict possible. Patrick Lencioni, in *The Five Dysfunctions of a Team*, pointed out that *fear of conflict* is often rooted in lack of trust. Establish trust, and teams can debate passionately without it getting personal.)

- Accountability and Reliability: When trust is present, people hold themselves and each other accountable in a positive way. If someone drops the ball, they own up to it, because they trust they won't be unfairly blamed or punished for an honest mistake. Likewise, teammates trust that others will do their part, so they don't feel the need to micromanage each other.
- Empathy and Understanding: Team members show care for one another. If someone is having a hard time personally or professionally, colleagues respond with support rather than exploiting the weakness. Empathy on a team means people feel "heard" and understood by one another. This sense of belonging further reinforces trust.

For a leader, building these elements starts with setting the tone. Akiro's case in Tokyo is a perfect example: by acknowledging his own missteps and explicitly stating trust in his people, he began to rewrite the team norms. Leaders are the thermostat of team culture – your behavior sets the temperature for trust or fear.

The Secure Leader: Confidence Without Ego

To effectively foster trust and empathy, a leader must operate from a place of security in themselves. This is where the idea of the secure leader comes in – essentially the evolved state of leadership after doing the inner work we discussed in previous chapters. A secure leader is comfortable in their own skin and position; they don't feel the need to constantly assert authority or prove they're the smartest in the room. This self- assurance allows them to lift others up rather than push them down.

One hallmark of secure leadership is what we might call confidence without ego . Secure leaders project confidence, but *they don't hog the spotlight or insist on being right.* They're comfortable delegating important tasks, trusting their team's abilities, and admitting when they don't know something. An insecure leader might perceive delegation as a threat ("what if my team member outshines me?"), but a secure leader sees it as a necessity for growth and success. By trusting their people, secure leaders actually *boost* team morale and accountability . Employees feel valued and take greater ownership of their work, leading to better outcomes for the organization.

Consider a practical scenario: imagine a manager who always has to have the final say versus one who often says, "I defer to the expert on this – what do you recommend?" The latter is likely a secure leader. By acknowledging someone else's expertise, they lose no authority; in fact, they gain respect. Their team sees that the leader's ego isn't a roadblock to progress. This in turn encourages team members to voice expertise and ideas more freely. It's a virtuous cycle – trust begets trust.

Here are a few key traits or behaviors commonly observed in secure leaders (you can use this as a mini checklist to assess or inspire your own behavior):

- They empower others. Secure leaders give power away – they empower their team through delegation, coaching, and giving credit where it's due. They're not threatened by the success of team members; in fact, they take pride in it. A secure leader might say, "My team's success *is* my success."

They maintain integrity and transparency. Being secure in oneself makes it easier to be honest and transparent. Secure leaders aren't afraid of the truth – even if it's bad news – and they don't feel a need to hide information to maintain control. This openness *fosters trust, leading to loyalty*. When you level with your team about challenges, they are more likely to rally with you because they trust you're not concealing things.

- They show vulnerability appropriately. As counterintuitive as it might sound, vulnerability is a strength for leaders. It humanizes you and builds trust. A secure leader is willing to say "I made a mistake" or "I need your help" because they're not paralyzed by fear of appearing weak. On the contrary, such admissions often *increase* others' trust in them – it signals authenticity and confidence. In Akiro's story, his admission of rigidity and his expression of trust were vulnerable moves that paid dividends in team trust.
- They are good listeners. Insecure leaders often can't truly listen; they're too busy crafting their response or defending their ego. Secure leaders, by contrast, listen to understand. They practice empathy in conversations, making people feel seen and heard. This skill alone dramatically elevates team trust. When team members feel their leader *hears* them, even if the leader ultimately decides against their suggestion, there is a baseline respect that keeps trust intact.
- They stay calm under pressure. Remember, a secure leader has healed much of their inner turmoil; they aren't likely to fly off the handle or panic in a crisis. This calmness is reassuring to a team. Knowing that the captain of the ship doesn't lose their cool in a storm helps everyone

stay focused. (We will address crisis leadership and resilience in the next chapter, but it's worth noting here that trust is reinforced when leaders handle pressure with grace – it proves reliability.)

Let's take a real-world insight: A 2024 Harvard Business Review article on high-performing teams emphasizes that "if you're like most seasoned leaders, you've heard a lot about the value of trust." It goes on to highlight that building trust is not a one-time event, but a continuous practice of behavior modeling.

The "mechanism" of creating a trusting culture, as one expert noted, is "modeling and rewarding acts of vulnerability." That is exactly what secure leaders excel at – they model the behaviors (like asking for feedback, admitting uncertainty) that signal trust, and they **reward those behaviors in others**. If an employee takes a principled risk or candidly identifies a problem, a secure leader commends them, reinforcing that trust and candor are valued.

Empathy: The Heart of Secure Leadership

Trust and empathy are twin pillars – trust is often thought of as cognitive (belief in someone's reliability or integrity) whereas empathy is more affective (feeling concern or understanding for someone's emotions). In practice, they reinforce each other. Demonstrating empathy builds trust, and a trusting environment enables greater empathy among its members.

Empathy in leadership means truly caring about your people – not just as "resources" or roles, but as human beings with aspirations, challenges, and feelings. It means striving to understand perspectives and experiences different from your own. A secure leader uses empathy to connect, motivate, and resolve issues in a humane way.

Recall Google's finding: the best teams consistently practiced empathy . Here's why empathy is so powerful in teams:

- Empathy validates people's experiences. When team members feel that their leader understands their point of view or at least respects it, they are more likely to trust that leader's decisions, even tough ones. Empathy doesn't mean always agreeing; it means communicating "I get how you feel and why you might feel that way." For example, telling a team member, "I realize this last-minute change is frustrating and I appreciate that you've had to work extra hours; I'm doing what I can to prevent this in the future" can turn resentment into cooperation.
- Empathy fosters loyalty and engagement. Leaders who show personal care – asking about an employee's sick child, remembering birthdays, or checking in when someone seems off – create strong bonds. People naturally reciprocate empathy with dedication. They'll go the extra mile not out of fear or obligation, but out of mutual respect and gratitude.
- Empathy improves communication. In a team with empathy, misunderstandings are reduced. People give each other the benefit of the doubt. If a terse email comes through, an empathetic culture leads someone to think "Maybe they're having a rough day" instead of immediately assuming ill intent. This prevents small frictions from escalating.
- Empathy drives inclusive decision-making. A leader who can empathize with various stakeholders (from entry-level employees to customers to investors) can make more informed and considerate decisions. Empathy broadens your view. It helps you anticipate how changes will impact people and therefore how best to implement those changes with minimal negative fallout.

How can you actively cultivate empathy as a leader? Here are a few strategies:

- Practice active listening – give your full attention in conversations, and reflect back what you hear. For instance, "It sounds like you're concerned about the timeline, is that right?" This validates the speaker and clarifies understanding.

Spend time with your team in their world – much like the nomikai in Tokyo, find informal or less hierarchical settings to interact. You could do periodic skip-level lunches (meeting with junior employees without their manager present) just to learn about them and their work. Or consider "walking the floor" regularly and chatting with folks. These interactions build rapport and give you insight into daily realities.

- Show you're willing to help – if you notice someone struggling, offer support. Even if they don't take it, the gesture matters. Saying, "I know you've been staying late; what can I do or authorize to make this easier?" shows you see and care about their effort.
- Be fair and consistent – favoritism or unpredictable moods destroy empathy because they create fear or resentment. Ensure you apply rules evenly and explain your decisions. When people feel fairly treated, they are more likely to empathize with *you* even when they disagree with your decisions.
- Encourage empathy within the team – set an expectation that teammates support each other. For example, if a team member is overwhelmed, you might ask others to pitch in and explicitly say, "We succeed or fail as a team." Also, model praising those who demonstrate kindness and teamwork, not just those who hit targets.

A vivid illustration of empathy in leadership comes from Indra Nooyi, the former CEO of PepsiCo. Nooyi was known for her extraordinary empathy and personal touch with employees. She famously wrote over 400 letters each year to the parents of her senior executives, praising them for the "gift" of their child's work and thanking them – a gesture of gratitude that deeply moved families . Nooyi said, *"I was a product of my upbringing... It occurred to me that I had never thanked the parents of my executives for the gift of their child to PepsiCo."* This highly personal leadership style made employees feel uniquely valued and seen not just as workers, but as people shaped by families and history. It's no surprise that under her tenure, PepsiCo consistently had high leadership approval ratings and strong performance. Nooyi's secure sense of self allowed her to lead with both head and heart, and it set a tone throughout the company that caring is compatible with competitiveness.

Building a High-Trust, High-Empathy Team: Practical Steps

Transforming a team culture doesn't happen overnight, but steady leader actions can make a big difference even within a few months. If you're looking to strengthen trust and empathy in your team, consider these practical steps and frameworks:

1. Set Clear Intentions and Norms: Be explicit with your team about the kind of culture you want to cultivate. In a team meeting, you might say, "I want us to operate with trust and openness. That means I encourage debate, I want you to call out issues early, and I have your back if things don't go as planned. In return, I ask that we all assume good intentions and support one another." By putting it in words, you create accountability for yourself and others. Some teams even create a charter or list of principles (e.g., "We challenge ideas, not people" or "It's safe to ask for help here") that everyone agrees to uphold.
2. Be the First to Trust: Leaders often wonder, "Should my team earn my trust or do I give trust first?" In high-trust cultures, leaders extend trust proactively. This might mean delegating a significant responsibility to someone as a vote of confidence, or sharing information widely by default (instead of hoarding it for a select few). Trust given often begets trust returned. Of course, use judgment – it's wise to trust but verify in critical matters – but err on the side of empowering your team. For example, if a team member comes with a proposal, instead of

micromanaging it, say "This sounds promising. I trust your judgment – run with it, and keep me posted on key updates."

3. Create Psychological Safety in Meetings: As leader, you are usually the highest status person in the room. People take cues from you on whether it's safe to speak. In meetings, deliberately hold back from being the first to give an opinion; ask others to weigh in first. When someone voices a dissent or bad news, thank them for it. Never shoot the messenger. Model active listening and reinforce contributions: "Thanks for raising that concern, that perspective is valuable." If you notice some individuals aren't speaking, invite them: "Alex, we haven't heard your view yet and I know you have experience in this area – what do you think?" However, avoid pouncing if they hesitate; the invitation should feel encouraging, not pressuring. Over time, these practices signal that the meeting room is a safe space for candor.
4. Encourage Vulnerability and Authenticity: One technique pioneered by some management workshops is for team members (leader included) to share personal stories or challenges, which can humanize everyone and build empathy. For instance, a team might have a session where each person talks about a value they learned from a past struggle. As the leader, you might share, "Early in my career, I was afraid to admit when I was overloaded, and I burned out. I learned that asking for help is not a weakness. So now I encourage you all – speak up if you're overwhelmed; we will figure it out together." When you open up, it often encourages others to do the same. It doesn't mean you must overshare or get excessively sentimental – you can stay professional – but showing some heart goes a long way.
5. Institute Regular Check-Ins and Feedback Loops: Trust is reinforced by communication. Consider brief weekly team check-ins (beyond task updates) where people can share how they're feeling about work. One method is the "Start-Stop-Continue" feedback exercise: ask each team member (including yourself) to say one thing they think the

team (or leadership) should start doing, one to stop doing, and one to continue. This invites constructive feedback and shows you as a leader are open to input on your own and the team's behavior. When someone offers a suggestion like "I think we should stop chastising departments publicly on email," treat that seriously rather than getting defensive; it's a trust-building opportunity to improve. Follow through on feasible suggestions, which shows you take their voice seriously.

6. Recognize and Address Trust Breaches: No team is perfect – there may be moments when trust is dented (a misunderstanding, a perceived unfair decision, etc.). Secure leaders tackle these incidents head- on with empathy and transparency. If you realize you broke trust (e.g., you promised to consult the team on a change but then didn't), own it: "I want to apologize for not getting your input on that policy change; I realize that went against our norm of inclusion. I'll explain why it happened and how I'll handle it differently next time." Such an apology can actually *strengthen* trust because it shows integrity. Similarly, if two team members have a conflict that's eroding trust, facilitate a resolution – perhaps bring them together, allow each to speak while the other listens, and help them find common ground or at least mutual respect. A team that sees their leader actively safeguarding the culture will feel more secure.
7. Continuous Learning and Adaptation: Building a trusting and empathetic team is an ongoing process. Solicit feedback about the team culture periodically: you can do anonymous surveys or have a third party run a focus group to gauge trust levels. Be ready to adapt your strategies based on what you learn. For example, if feedback indicates that remote team members feel less included, you might institute new communication norms or virtual team-building specifically to bridge that gap. Show the team that their well-being and cohesion are a top priority and that you're willing to learn and improve as a leader to support that.

The Outcomes of Trust and Empathy

It's worth painting a picture of what you stand to gain by investing in trust and empathy. When a team reaches a high level of trust, several wonderful things happen:

- Speed and Agility: Decision-making accelerates because people aren't bogged down in approval layers or CYA (cover-your-ass) behaviors. In a high-trust environment, if an issue arises, the first instinct is to *fix the problem*, not *fix the blame*. That saves enormous time and energy. Also, team members will more readily adjust roles or jump in to help each other, making the group more agile in responding to change.
- Innovation: New ideas flow more freely. People dare to think outside the box because they aren't afraid of ridicule for suggesting something unconventional. We often hear that diversity drives innovation – but diversity only works if there's an inclusive, trusting atmosphere where diverse perspectives are truly heard. Secure leaders create that space, and the result is often a boom in creativity.
- Resilience to Setbacks: A trusting team can weather storms far better. If something fails, they pull together rather than fall apart. They trust that leadership will be honest about the situation and that they won't be unfairly punished for setbacks, so they channel their energy into solutions. Empathy among team members means they support each other through crunch times, preventing burnout and improving retention.

Employee Development and Retention: People in high-trust teams tend to grow faster. Why? Because they are more open about what they need to learn, and they get candid feedback in a helpful way. Mentoring and peer coaching flourish in such an environment. Furthermore, talented folks tend to stay where they feel valued and trusted. A study in *Harvard Business Review* noted that people at high-trust companies reported significantly less stress and higher engagement than those at low-trust companies. In an era where retaining top talent is critical, trust isn't just a "soft" thing – it has hard dollar implications in terms of turnover costs and performance.

To circle back to Akiro's Tokyo team: after that project, the firm noticed that the division's employee engagement scores jumped in their annual survey. Not only that, but client satisfaction on projects handled by Akiro's team improved too. It seemed that the culture of trust internally was spilling over into better service externally – employees were more proactive and collaborative in solving client issues. This is a common observation: a strong, trusting internal culture becomes visible to customers and partners in positive ways (and conversely, a toxic internal culture is hard to hide from the outside world).

Akiro's personal leadership journey also evolved. He became known within the company as a "secure base" leader – a term coined by leadership expert George Kohlrieser to describe leaders who provide a sense of safety and care (the "base") while also encouraging challenge and risk-taking (the "secure" part). Essentially, a secure base leader gives people confidence to explore and innovate, because they know support is there if they falter. This concept ties wonderfully with trust and empathy: you as a leader act as that base of trust, and with empathy you give people the courage to stretch.

Trust and Empathy: Diagnostics for Leaders

Let's include a brief self-assessment to wrap up this chapter. Reflect on the following questions to evaluate how well you're building trust and empathy:

- Do team members freely bring up bad news or admit mistakes to me? Or do I often hear about problems only when it's too late (a sign people were afraid to speak up)?

- In team discussions, what percentage of the talking do I do? (If it's most of it, consider pulling back to listen more. If it's balanced with others, that's a good sign.)
- Can I name personal aspirations or challenges for each of my direct reports? (This gauges how well you know them as individuals – which correlates with empathy.)
- When I last received tough feedback, how did I respond? (Did I thank the person and consider it, or get defensive? Your response will either reinforce or erode the trust for giving honest feedback.)
- Do I delegate important tasks, or do I frequently find myself saying "I'll just do it"? (Over-control can signal lack of trust in others and stifle their growth. Aim to delegate and then support, rather than micromanage.)
- How do I handle conflicts in the team? (Do I avoid them, or address them openly and fairly? A secure leader with trust present will facilitate resolution in a way that people feel heard and treated justly.)
- Would my team members say I have their best interests at heart? (This one you might have to intuit or gather from subtle feedback. But it's the ultimate empathy question – if the majority would say "Yes, I do feel my boss cares about me," you're on the right track.)

Building trust and empathy is truly a leader's art form. It blends emotional intelligence, communication skills, and consistent integrity. The payoff, however, is immense – not just in performance metrics, but in the sheer satisfaction of leading a team that has your back as much as you have theirs. There's a joy in that kind of work environment that makes the hard days easier to bear and the victories far sweeter.

As we look ahead, keep in mind that even a high-trust team will face inevitable pressures: deadlines, conflicts, external crises, personal stresses. The next chapter will explore how a leader and their team can handle pressure, conflict, and stress while maintaining the trust and empathy we've established. We will delve into the qualities of resilience and learn how to emerge stronger from the fires that leadership throws our way. With the foundation of a secure, trusting culture, you are already stacking the odds in favor of resilient performance. Now, let's examine how to further cultivate resilience when the heat is on.

CHAPTER 12

UNDER PRESSURE – CONFLICT, STRESS, AND THE RESILIENT LEADER

Opening Story: A Founder's Fire in Nairobi

Natasha leaned against the railing of her startup's rooftop terrace in Nairobi, watching the dusk settle over the city. In the distance, beyond the skyline, a plume of dark smoke curled upwards – a literal fire was raging somewhere in the industrial area. It felt symbolic, because *inside* her, everything seemed to be burning down too. Natasha was the founder of a social enterprise that provided solar-powered lamps to off-grid communities in Kenya. What started as a passionate venture with a small team of idealists had grown into a 50-person organization. But growth brought pressure. That week, Natasha's venture was grappling with a serious conflict: her operations manager, David, and her head of sales, Joyce, were locked in a feud over inventory shortages that led to missed deliveries. The sales team accused ops of poor planning; ops shot back that sales consistently over-promised to clients. The tension had escalated into a shouting match in a meeting that afternoon, right in front of Natasha. She had tried to mediate, but both David and Joyce were entrenched and looking to her to take sides. To top it off, a major investor was scheduled to visit in two days for a performance review, and these internal fractures were threatening to derail the company's image and, frankly, its functionality.

As a leader, Natasha felt the squeeze from all sides – loyalty to her team members, responsibility to the investors and community, and her own internal standards (not to mention fatigue; she hadn't slept well in weeks). The weight of stress bore down heavily. Part of her just wanted to scream into the Nairobi night, to release the frustration. But part of her – the resilient part she had been cultivating – took a deep breath instead. "This is a fire I have to walk through," she whispered to herself. "My team is watching how I handle this. I need to be the steady one now, even if I don't feel it inside."

The next morning, Natasha called an emergency meeting with her leadership team. Instead of immediately addressing the conflict between David and Joyce, she did something unexpected: she shared *her own state of mind*. "I won't lie, I feel like we're under immense pressure, and it's been hard on me too," she admitted. "I woke up at 4 AM worrying about our delivery issues and this investor visit. But I realized fighting each other isn't going to solve it. We all care about this mission, and we're all stressed. Let's start from that point – acknowledging that we're in this together – and then figure our way out." Her openness took the edge off the room. David and Joyce both looked slightly embarrassed, suddenly aware that their battle had added to the strain rather than alleviating it.

Natasha then facilitated a problem-solving session. She set some ground rules: *focus on the problem, not the person; no blame, only accountability*. They mapped out the supply chain on a whiteboard and pinpointed where communication broke down between sales and ops. It became clear that both departments had valid points – there were indeed stock issues from a supplier delay (ops' domain) and some overestimation of delivery capacity in client deals (sales' domain). Rather than dwell on past mistakes, Natasha guided them to create a rapid response plan: a temporary reallocation of inventory, a jointly signed letter to affected clients with an apology and revised delivery dates, and a daily huddle between David and Joyce for the next two weeks to ensure alignment.

At one moment, David muttered, "Maybe I am not cut out for this pace," expressing doubt in the heat of problem-solving. Joyce, having calmed down, responded empathetically, "We're all learning as we go. I'm sorry I threw your team under the bus. Let's fix it together." Natasha noted the change – this was the first time in weeks she'd seen them show understanding toward each other. By the end of the meeting, there was a tangible sense of relief. A plan was in motion, and more importantly, the two warring colleagues had found common ground, forged by the shared realization that *the enemy was the problem, not each other.*

The investor visit came and went; Natasha navigated it with transparency about their challenges and the corrective actions underway. The investor appreciated the candor and the clear steps being taken – in fact, he remarked that seeing the team handle a tough situation gave him more confidence than any smooth presentation could have. Over the ensuing months, the startup stabilized its operations. But more than the operational fixes, what remained with Natasha and her team was the lesson in resilience. They had faced a conflict and a high-stress crisis without falling apart. Instead of finger-pointing, they practiced problem-solving; instead of panic, they fostered communication. It wasn't easy – resilience rarely is – but it left them stronger and better prepared for the next curveball.

The Nature of Pressure: Leaders in the Crucible

Leadership is often forged in what Warren Bennis called "crucible experiences" – moments of extreme challenge or adversity that test what you're made of. Conflict, stress, and pressure are inevitable in any leadership journey. Projects will go awry, personalities will clash, markets will shift, crises will erupt (from a server meltdown to a global pandemic).

The difference between teams that crumble and those that thrive under pressure often boils down to one quality: resilience.

So what is resilience? It's commonly defined as the ability to bounce back from setbacks, to adapt, and to keep going in the face of adversity. Professor George Kohlrieser describes resilience as *"the human capacity to meet adversity, setbacks and trauma, and then recover from them in order to live life fully."* In leadership terms, resilience means you can sustain your energy and clarity under pressure, cope with disruptive changes, and "overcome major difficulties without engaging in dysfunctional behavior or harming others." That last part is crucial – anyone can appear "tough" by lashing out or shutting down emotionally, but a resilient leader navigates turmoil *without* leaving a trail of broken trust or burnt bridges.

Resilient leadership is both a mindset and a skillset:

- Mindset: A resilient leader typically has an optimistic yet realistic outlook. They believe problems are solvable, challenges contain lessons, and no matter how bad today is, tomorrow can be better through effort or ingenuity. This often aligns with having a growth mindset – seeing abilities and situations as improvable rather than fixed. They ask "How can we make this work?" instead of declaring defeat. Importantly, they don't see adversity as a personal indictment, but as a natural part of the journey to overcome.
- Skillset: Resilient leaders employ specific strategies to handle stress and conflict. These include emotional regulation techniques (like Natasha taking a deep breath and steadying herself), effective conflict resolution skills, clear communication under duress, and the ability to reframe problems in a way that points to action rather than despair (Natasha reframed "we're doomed" to "we have a hard problem, but we'll tackle it together").

Let's talk about conflict first, as a common pressure point. Conflict in a team or organization is unavoidable – in fact, as we noted in Chapter 11, some conflict is healthy for innovation and airing diverse views. The goal is not a conflict-free team (which might indicate apathy or artificial harmony), but rather a team that handles conflict constructively. A resilient leader leans into conflict when it matters, rather than avoiding it. As one guide from Harvard notes, avoiding conflict is costly – unresolved conflicts can cost organizations huge amounts in lost productivity and morale. Indeed, one study found that American companies lose an estimated $359 billion annually due to the impact of unresolved workplace conflict. Additionally, over half of employees (in one poll, 53%) admitted to handling "toxic" situations by avoiding them – essentially kicking the can down the road, which often makes things worse.

Resilient leadership in conflict means: - Recognizing conflict early and impartially. - Creating a safe space (leveraging that trust culture we discussed) for the parties to air issues. - Facilitating understanding: often simply letting each side explain their perspective fully can de-escalate tension as misunderstandings are cleared. - Finding common goals: e.g., "We all want the project to succeed, we just differ on approach." -

Encouraging a *problem-solving* orientation: focus on what to do next, not just what went wrong. - Knowing when to compromise and when to stand firm on principles. (This is nuanced; not all conflicts are symmetric – sometimes one party is in the wrong ethically or performance-wise, and resilience also means taking decisive action. For example, if a team member is acting in bad faith or toxicity, a resilient leader doesn't endlessly accommodate that; they address it head-on, which could mean role reassignment or even letting the person go, but done in a fair, documentation-supported way.)

Now consider stress and pressure at the individual level for a leader. The higher you climb, the more responsibility and visibility, which often means more stress. Leadership stress can come from overwork, high stakes decisions, public scrutiny, uncertainty, and, yes, conflicts like Natasha faced. Chronic stress can erode decision-making, creativity, and health if not managed. The resilient leader, therefore, is one who develops strong stress-management habits. They treat resilience like physical fitness – something to be maintained through consistent practices.

A few evidence-based practices for building personal resilience are: - Mindfulness or meditation: Training your mind to find calm can improve your ability to stay composed under fire. Even simple deep-breathing techniques during a tense moment can lower your physiological stress response (heart rate, cortisol, etc.), preventing you from reacting impulsively. - Reframing and cognitive agility: This means altering your mental narrative about a stressor. Psychologist Viktor Frankl famously wrote about the freedom to choose one's attitude in any given set of circumstances. For a leader, reframing could be seeing a market downturn not as "we're sunk" but as "an opportunity to pivot and serve customers differently." Reframing doesn't deny the reality; it searches for a useful way to respond to it . In our story, Natasha reframed the internal conflict from "a personal feud" to "a shared stress we can solve together," which allowed collaborative action. - Support systems: Resilient leaders don't go it alone. They have coaches, mentors, peers, or friends they can confide in and seek counsel from. Sometimes just talking about what you're facing with someone you trust (maintaining confidentiality where needed) can prevent you from feeling isolated with the weight of the world. In a team context, a resilient organization fosters peer support – colleagues who step up for each other. As a leader, don't hesitate to draw on your support network. It's not a weakness; it's strategic. Also consider professional support: coaches or therapists can provide an external perspective and coping tools for high stress. - Self-care basics: Sleep, exercise, nutrition – these are often the first casualties in a high- pressure phase, but they are exactly what fortify you to handle pressure. Arianna Huffington wrote extensively about how her leadership improved when she prioritized sleep after a severe burnout episode. Physical resilience feeds mental resilience. Think of stress as drawing down from a bank account of energy; self-care deposits back into that account. A tired, malnourished, burnt-out leader will struggle to be resilient or make good decisions. - Setting boundaries: Paradoxically, resilient leaders know when to say no or protect their team's focus. If every demand or crisis gets an immediate yes, you'll exhaust your resources. Sometimes resilience means pushing back on unreasonable timelines or juggling priorities rather than trying to do it all at once. For instance, a resilient project manager might renegotiate a deadline with a client when an unforeseen issue arises, rather than drive the team to a breaking point. Boundaries also apply to maintaining personal time – an evening off, a weekend with family – which give mental recovery so you can be effective when back on duty.

Resilience in Action: Conflict to Collaboration

To further illustrate conflict resolution and resilience, let's outline a general approach a leader can take when conflicts flare (adaptable to many situations):

1. ***Set the Stage (Psychological Safety):*** Just as Natasha did by sharing her feelings, start by creating a non-threatening environment. You might call a meeting in a neutral location or even outside the usual office setting. Acknowledge the conflict and express your intention: *"I know there's a conflict around X. My goal isn't to blame anyone but to find a solution that works and to ensure we remain a strong team."* This reinforces that *the team staying intact and effective* is as important as solving the issue at hand.
2. ***Listen to Each Perspective:*** Allow each party to speak, one at a time, without interruption. It can be helpful to have a guideline like "each of you will get the floor for a few minutes – the other(s) will listen

actively, then we'll summarize what we heard." As a leader, model *active listening*: nod, take notes, and paraphrase what each person said to ensure they feel heard. Often, being heard and understood (even if there's disagreement) significantly lowers the emotional temperature. It's like letting steam out of a pressure cooker.

3. ***Identify the Root Causes:*** Many conflicts are symptoms of underlying issues. Use a coaching approach – ask open-ended questions: "What do you think is really causing the missed targets?" or "How did we get here, from your viewpoint?" Sometimes it might be a process failure, ambiguous roles, or external stress. By pinpointing the root (lack of resources, miscommunication, misaligned goals, personality clash, etc.), you can address the real problem. If emotions run high during this, help the group focus by writing the issues on a whiteboard or shared document – externalizing them as problems to solve collectively.
4. ***Find Areas of Agreement:*** Even warring parties usually agree on something. It might be as basic as "we both care about the project's success" or "we both feel frustrated and want this situation resolved." Acknowledge those aloud. This establishes a collaborative tone: *we have shared interests*. In Natasha's case, both David and Joyce cared about customer satisfaction and the company's mission. Reminding them of that helped unite them on the same side of the table, metaphorically.
5. ***Brainstorm Solutions Together:*** Encourage everyone (including you) to suggest ideas to resolve the conflict or mitigate the issue. At this stage, quantity over quality – get all ideas out without immediate evaluation. This transitions the energy from confrontation to co-creation. In doing so, you're also subtly teaching the team to use problem-solving as the default response to conflict rather than finger-pointing. Once ideas are on the table, discuss the pros/cons of each and converge on a plan.

6. ***Agree on Actions and Accountability:*** Resilience is built not just in talk, but in follow-through. Clearly outline who will do what, by when, to address the situation. Also, consider what mechanisms will prevent recurrence. This might involve new processes (like the daily huddle between sales and ops that Natasha implemented), or setting norms ("in future, if X happens, we agree to inform each other immediately rather than let resentment build"). Ensure each party commits to the solution. Sometimes, a neutral facilitator (you or a third party) might check in on the progress periodically.
7. ***Learn and Document the Lesson:*** After the dust settles, a resilient leader captures the learning. This could be a brief write-up of "what we learned from the Q3 incident" to share with a wider team so everyone gains wisdom from it. Or it could simply be a team debrief meeting: *"Now that we've come through this challenge, what did we do well and what can we improve next time we face a tough situation?"* By doing this, you normalize learning from conflict and stress rather than avoiding discussing it. The team thus internalizes that *conflict and crises are opportunities to grow stronger.* This is essentially the concept of antifragility (coined by Nassim Nicholas Taleb) – the idea that some systems benefit from shocks/stressors and come back stronger, not just bouncing back to the same level.

Natasha's team, for instance, emerged more cohesive. By weathering that storm, David and Joyce actually developed mutual respect. Experiencing firsthand that they could argue vehemently and still work it out likely made them less fearful of future disagreements – a hallmark of resilience.

Leading Under Extreme Stress: The Resilient Mindset

In high stakes situations – think crisis leadership, like a PR scandal, a tragic accident, or a sudden massive business disruption – leaders often have to be the emotional anchor for others while managing their own stress. It's like being the eye of the storm: calm at the center while chaos whirls around. Here are some tips for those extreme moments:

- ***Communicate, Communicate, Communicate:*** In crises, uncertainty is what breeds panic. A resilient leader *over-communicates* to counteract rumors and fear. Be as transparent as possible about what's happening, what is known/unknown, and what's being done. During a crisis, people look to leaders for cues; going silent or vague usually worsens anxiety. Even if you don't have all the answers, saying "Here's what we know, here's what we're doing, and we'll update you in 2 hours" is far better than a void. Clarity is a component of resilience at the organizational level.
- ***Project Calm Confidence:*** This doesn't mean false optimism or denying reality. It means modulating your tone and body language to be steady. A trembling voice or panicked expressions will amplify fear in others. If needed, take a moment in private to collect yourself (breathing exercises, a quick consult with a trusted colleague, etc.) so that when you face your team, you can be the composed leader they need. As one Navy SEAL saying goes, *"Calm is contagious."* If you remain calm, it helps others regain their composure.
- ***Triage and Prioritize:*** In high stress, there may be a hundred things demanding attention. Resilient leaders quickly figure out what's most critical (safety, stopping losses, etc.) and what can wait. This is analogous to battlefield triage or ER triage – address life-threatening issues first, then handle the rest in order. Delegating is crucial here: assign task forces or individuals to handle specific streams of work. This not only distributes the load, but also gives people a sense of agency rather than helplessness.
- ***Take Care of Your People:*** Under heavy stress, remember that your team members are humans, not just roles. Check in on them: Are they getting rest? Do they need a break? Sometimes in a crunch, people

won't pause unless a leader explicitly says "Take a 30-minute break, we need you fresh." Show empathy for the pressure they're under, and celebrate small wins or progress to keep morale up. A simple, "Thank you for pulling together" in the midst of a crisis can bolster spirits.

- ***Keep Perspective:*** This is hard in the heat of the moment, but try to contextualize the situation. Ask yourself, "What's the worst that will realistically happen? Can we handle that? What might matter about this one year from now?" Such questions can reduce a tendency to catastrophize. Often, even if the worst outcome is bad, recognizing it and having a contingency plan can relieve some dread because you transform fear of the unknown into a concrete scenario you can tackle. Also, recall past challenges you overcame as a team – it reminds everyone, *we've been through tough times and came out okay.*
- ***Be Willing to Make Tough Decisions:*** Resilient leadership isn't always about being nice; it's about being brave and values-driven. Sometimes you have to make a call under uncertainty. Maybe you have to decide to pivot a strategy entirely on short notice, or to cut a project to save resources for another – these can be gut-wrenching. Use your best judgment, consult advisors if possible, but then own the decision. Indecisiveness prolongs pain. In a pressure scenario, making a decision and committing to it (while remaining agile to adjust if new info comes) is usually better than analysis paralysis.
- ***Self-Reflection Post-Crisis:*** After making it through, do a personal debrief. How did you handle it? What did you learn about yourself? Resilient leaders are forged in those crucibles, but only if they process and integrate the lessons. Maybe you discovered you have a temper trigger you need to manage better, or perhaps you found that your intuition in crisis is usually right and you'll trust it more next time. This continuous improvement mindset ensures each challenge increases your resilience.

The Resilient Leader's Toolkit: Checklist and Practices

Let's consolidate some key takeaways in a practical way. Below is a Resilient Leader's Toolkit – a quick checklist/reminder of practices for conflict, stress, and resilience:

- Emotional Regulation Techniques: Have at least one go-to method to center yourself (e.g., deep breathing, counting, short walk, mindfulness app) when you feel stress surging. Use it proactively.
- "Pause" Button: In conflict or heated moments, don't be afraid to call a short break. A few minutes can prevent saying or doing things in anger. Encourage others to use this too (e.g., "Let's pause and reconvene in 10 minutes with cooler heads").
- Language of Resolution: Use "we" language and solution-focused words. Instead of "You did

X" (blame), say "We are facing X challenge, how shall we solve it?" Avoid absolute terms like "always" or "never" when addressing issues; they put people on defense.

- Perspective-Taking: In conflict, challenge yourself to argue from the other person's viewpoint. This can reveal areas of compromise or at least help you empathize and reduce personal animosity.
- Hydration and Breath: Under stress, people often literally forget basics like drinking water or breathing fully. Keep water at hand in long crises. Occasionally do a breath exercise with your team (it might feel strange, but even saying "Everyone take a deep breath" can inject a tiny moment of calm).
- Time-Out for Big Decisions: If circumstances allow, avoid making major decisions at the peak of stress or when emotions are hot. Even a overnight sleep on it can bring clarity. Resilient decisions are often timely but not hasty.

- Conflict Playbook: If not already established, create a simple team protocol for disagreements. For example: 1) address issues directly with the person involved one-on-one first, 2) if unresolved, involve a neutral third party (maybe a manager or HR), 3) focus on specific behaviors/facts, not personal attacks, 4) propose at least one solution when raising a problem. Having this playbook can guide people to handle conflicts more systematically and less emotionally.
- Stress Outlets: Encourage healthy outlets. Maybe have a "walk and talk" meeting instead of sitting in a tense conference room, or initiate a casual team run or yoga session during stressful project push (if the team is open to it). Physically moving can dispel stress hormones and clear minds – don't underestimate it.
- Humor (When Appropriate): Humor can be a relief valve if used sensitively (never to mock someone's concern). A shared laugh can remind everyone of our shared humanity. Resilient teams often have inside jokes born from tough times – it shows they can find light even when things are dark. Just ensure the humor is inclusive, not at someone's expense.
- Acknowledgment of Effort: During and after a high-pressure period, acknowledge the hard work and sacrifices made. Recognition fuels resilience because people feel their pain had purpose and was seen. This could be as simple as a heartfelt thank-you speech, or a team lunch, or giving comp time off after a crunch.
- Know Your "Why": Often forgotten, but central to resilience, is remembering the purpose behind the struggle. When things go awry, remind yourself and your team why you're doing what you do. In Natasha's case, it was the mission to bring light to communities. Recalling that can ignite intrinsic motivation to push through challenges. It provides a reason to endure and adapt.

Emerging Stronger: The Gift of Adversity

It might sound Pollyanna to call adversity a gift, but many seasoned leaders reflect that their toughest trials shaped them far more than their easy wins. Conflict teaches the value of communication and compromise; stress teaches limits and priorities; failure teaches humility and innovation. In the scope of "The Leader Was Once a Child," think about how childhood adversity, once healed, became a source of empathy and strength. Similarly, organizational adversity, once overcome, becomes a source of confidence and unity.

A team that has navigated a crisis successfully often carries a quiet confidence: "We faced down that storm, we can handle the next." It's like how veterans of a difficult campaign share a bond and a belief in each other. As a leader, each time you guide your team through pressure without breaking, you reinforce that culture of resilience. It doesn't mean you seek out stress for its own sake, but you no longer need to fear it.

Natasha's story in Nairobi didn't end with that conflict resolution. A year later, her company faced another trial – a sudden government policy change affecting import tariffs on solar equipment, which threatened their cost structure. It was a big external challenge. But this time, her team responded differently than they might have a year before. Instead of panic, they gathered, shared concerns openly (no more siloed finger- pointing between departments), and brainstormed adaptations – including sourcing some components locally and rallying a coalition of similar enterprises to lobby for a policy revision. The tariff issue took months to resolve, but they stayed cohesive and even managed to turn it into a positive PR story about supporting local manufacturing. David and Joyce, once bitter rivals, co-led the internal task force managing this change, exemplifying cross-functional solidarity.

This highlights an encouraging point: resilience begets resilience. Over time, you are not just solving one problem after another; you are building a *capability* within yourself and your organization to absorb and adapt to whatever comes. It's like a muscle that strengthens with each use. Early in your career, a single tough client might stress you for days; later, you might be juggling a merger integration and a PR crisis with far more composure, because you've grown.

In concluding this chapter, consider how the themes of transformation converge here. The leader who was once a child – perhaps a child who faced struggles – has now transformed those wounds into wisdom (Chapter 10's healing), gained clarity of vision (Chapter 9), created bonds of trust (Chapter 11), and with those in place, can withstand pressure (Chapter 12). It's a journey from vulnerability to strength, not by avoiding challenges, but by confronting and learning from them.

As we move to the Conclusion, keep in mind the image of the leader you needed as a child. Often, that leader is someone who provides safety, understanding, and inspiration during tough times. By developing your resilience and leading your team with trust and empathy through conflicts and stress, you are very much becoming that kind of leader. You become the steady hand, the encouraging voice, the problem- solver, the protector. You demonstrate to those you lead (and to your inner younger self) that challenges can be met with courage and compassion. No matter what pressures come, the resilient leader's mantra is captured well in an old proverb: *"Smooth seas do not make skillful sailors."* You and your team can face the rough seas, and when the waters calm, you'll not only reach the shore but do so with greater skill, confidence, and unity than before.

Conclusion: Be the Leader You Needed as a Child

"You can't go back and change your childhood. But you can lead in a way that heals it." These words – first mentioned to you at the start of this journey – carry even more weight now that we've traversed the landscape of transformation together. In Part III, we explored how rewriting your leadership story, healing old wounds, building trust, and developing resilience all converge toward a powerful outcome: becoming the kind of leader that your younger self (and others' younger selves) would look up to. In essence, to be the leader you needed as a child is to embody the guidance, support, and inspiration that perhaps you once lacked or yearned for. It's the culmination of personal transformation into a force for good in the lives of those you lead.

The Journey Revisited: From Child to Transformational Leader

Let's briefly reflect on the arc we've traveled:

- In Chapter 9, we met Eduardo in São Paulo, awakening to the insight that he didn't have to be chained to an old story of fear. We learned to harness personal insight to craft a compelling vision. This taught us the value of authenticity and purpose in leadership – that our life stories, even the painful parts, can inform a vision that is uniquely ours and genuinely inspiring to others. We practiced writing our own leadership narrative, turning hindsight into foresight.
- In Chapter 10, through Aarav's story in Pune, we confronted the "inner child." Healing old wounds – the perfectionism, the insecurities, the need for approval – was not about indulgence but about liberation. We saw how addressing those issues made Aarav not only happier and more whole, but a far more effective and compassionate leader. We discovered tools for self-healing (from listening to our inner child to reparenting ourselves) and saw how an empowered leader emerges when the leader's younger self is no longer driving out of fear, but the adult self is driving with wisdom.
- In Chapter 11, Akiro in Tokyo showed us the fruits of that inner work – the secure leader who can build trust and empathy in a team.

We broke down how trust accelerates performance and how empathy binds teams together. We explored practical ways to be that secure base for others: delegating, listening, showing vulnerability and integrity. Akiro's transformation from a distant authority to an approachable, trusting leader demonstrated how secure leadership creates a culture where people thrive and dare to be their best.

- In Chapter 12, Natasha in Nairobi put everything to the test under pressure. Conflict, stress, and crises are the exams of leadership, and a leader who has done the prior work is far better equipped to ace them. We learned strategies for conflict resolution and stress management, and we witnessed how a leader's resilience can literally turn fire into growth. Natasha's ability to rally her team through turmoil without breaking them – and in fact strengthening them – was a vivid example of *responsive, empathetic leadership under pressure.*

Now, standing at the end of Part III, the theme "Transformation" shines clearly. Each chapter addressed a dimension of personal change that enables a leader to transform not just themselves but their impact on others. If Part I of this book (not in this text, but implied) was perhaps about understanding your inner child and Part II about nurturing it, Part III was about truly leading with that integrated self – turning personal mastery into organizational leadership.

The Leader You Needed

Take a moment to remember the younger version of you – perhaps the 8-year-old who dreamed big but was afraid of the dark, or the teenager who struggled to fit in, or the junior employee who felt lost in a big corporate machine. Who did that person need?

Maybe it was someone who would listen without judgment, someone who would say "I believe in you," someone who modeled courage and kindness, someone who made you feel safe to take risks, or someone who simply noticed you. Many of us carry a mental image of a teacher, a relative, a coach, or even a fictional hero who provided that spark or safety at some point. But many also carry a wish that *there had been* such a figure at certain crossroads where there was none.

Being the leader you needed as a child means filling that role for others now. It means you strive to be the boss who recognizes potential in a shy team member and mentors them, because you remember being overlooked. It means you strive to cultivate a team atmosphere of trust and play, because you remember the stiffness or fear in a past job and how it stifled you. It means when someone makes a mistake, you respond with the firm-but-kind guidance you wish a parent or elder had shown you when you erred, turning it into a teachable moment instead of humiliation.

In concrete terms, consider these manifestations of "the leader you needed":

- If you needed encouragement – Now, you give encouragement. You catch people doing things right and acknowledge it. You become a confidence builder.
- If you needed patience – Now, you practice patience. You allow people time to learn, to fail and try again, as long as they're making progress. You don't snap at the first misstep.
- If you needed autonomy – Now, you grant trust and autonomy. You don't micromanage every detail but give people space to own their work, stepping in to guide rather than control.
- If you needed fairness – Now, you ensure fairness. You address favoritism, you make sure credit is given where due, you strive to be just and even-handed, remembering how demoralizing unfair treatment can be.
- If you needed understanding – Now, you are empathetic. When an employee is struggling personally, you respond with compassion and

flexibility if possible, not with scorn. You recall when you felt alone with a problem and vow that those under your leadership won't feel that way if you can help it.

- If you needed a role model – Now, you exemplify the values you talk about. You demonstrate integrity, or courage, or balance, or whatever you once admired and sought in others. By doing so, you become that source of inspiration for someone else.

None of this implies perfection. Indeed, part of being the leader you needed is being open about imperfection – showing that it's okay to be human and learning. Remember our discussions on vulnerability: a leader who admits they don't know everything or owns up to mistakes is likely exactly the kind of authentic figure many of us wish we saw growing up. Authenticity is magnetic. As you embody these traits, you heal not only yourself but potentially others who might have similar wounds or gaps from their past.

Healing Forward: The Ripple Effect of Your Leadership

One profound realization many leaders come to is that leadership is a form of service. By leading others, you have the opportunity to positively influence lives. When you lead in a way that "heals" – in a way that provides care, structure, and empowerment – you might be helping others mend their own past challenges, or at least not repeat the pains of the past.

For instance, think of a new graduate on your team, anxious about their performance. Under a fear-based manager, they might develop insecurities or unhealthy stress. But under a leader who coaches and supports, that young professional might blossom with confidence and skill. They, in turn, may lead others in the same supportive way down the line. This is the ripple effect of leadership.

Understanding that each team member is essentially "a child who grew up" (with their own backstory, hopes, and fears) can change the way you lead them. You begin to lead the *whole person*, not just the employee. You might be the one who encourages someone to pursue a talent they were shy about, or who convinces someone to not give up after a failure, or who guides someone through a conflict towards reconciliation.

There's a term in psychology: re-parenting. It's the idea that through therapy or relationships, one can symbolically give an adult what they missed as a child in terms of validation, love, or guidance. As a leader, you're not a therapist or a parent in the literal sense, but you do hold a role of authority and care that can reframe someone's negative past experiences with authority. If someone had a demeaning parent or a biased teacher, being a fair and uplifting leader can, in a way, rewrite their narrative about what people in authority can be. It shows them a positive model and perhaps heals a little bit of that old wound by experience.

A quick real-world example: Satya Nadella, CEO of Microsoft, is often cited for his empathetic leadership. His personal story of caring for his child with special needs deeply shaped his approach to leadership – prioritizing empathy, accessibility, and a growth mindset in Microsoft's culture. Employees frequently note how different the culture became under his "kinder, more listening" style compared to the prior more combative culture . Nadella, in a sense, became the kind of leader that fosters learning and well-being, not just intense competition. Under his leadership, many who might have burned out or felt stifled in the old culture found room to grow and express themselves. The result? Microsoft saw a renaissance in innovation and employee engagement. This is not coincidence – it's transformation in action.

By leading with transformation – insight, healing, trust, resilience – you not only drive results, you also contribute to the human growth of those around you. And that is a legacy that endures beyond any quarterly report.

A Continuing Journey

While this may be the end of the book, your journey of leadership is ongoing. Transformation is not a one- and-done deal; it's a continuous evolution. The leader you are today can continue to mature, to adapt to new challenges, to deepen in wisdom and compassion. As the world changes, new insights will be needed, new wounds may surface (or old ones in new forms), new levels of trust will have to be built, and resilience will be tested in unforeseen ways. But you have a framework now – a way of approaching leadership growth that is self-aware and people-aware.

Remember the diagnostic checklists, the frameworks, and the stories shared in these chapters. They are tools you can revisit whenever you feel off-course. Perhaps a few years from now, you'll catch yourself slipping into an old script or noticing a new trigger; that's the moment to do an Insight to Vision reset, or an inner child check-in. Maybe you'll join a new organization with low trust; that's the time to intentionally practice those trust-building steps from scratch. Or you might face an unprecedented crisis (as many did in 2020 with the pandemic); that's when to draw on your resilience toolkit and lead your team through with transparency and courage.

Leading as the leader you needed also implies mentorship. Consider paying it forward by guiding the next generation of leaders in these principles. Encourage them to reflect on their stories, to value emotional intelligence as much as technical skills, to build cultures of trust, and to not shy away from vulnerability. In doing so, you propagate a healthier, more human-centered leadership ethos in whatever domain you're in – corporate, startup, non-profit, government, community.

The Child Within the Leader

One beautiful irony of this journey is that as you become the leader you needed, you also finally give *your own inner child* what they needed. By showing patience to others, you inherently must be patient with yourself. By championing others' growth, you affirm your own capacity to grow. By creating a safe environment for your team, you end up working in a safe environment – which benefits you as well. It's a virtuous cycle.

Think back to Eduardo peering out over São Paulo, Aarav in the temple in Pune, Akiro raising a toast in Tokyo, Natasha taking a breath on the rooftop in Nairobi. Each of them, in those transformative moments, was not only leading others differently, but also quietly healing themselves. Eduardo's new vision gave meaning to his father's struggle, Aarav's change freed him from his father's harsh voice in his head, Akiro's trust-building likely redeemed some of the rigidity he grew up with in hierarchical culture, and Natasha's compassionate yet firm crisis leadership perhaps gave her the confidence that even in chaos, she could provide the steadiness she once wished for.

Their stories are fictional composites, but they mirror real patterns many leaders experience. And you, writing your own leadership story, are now equipped to navigate those patterns with insight and intentionality.

A Final Inspiring Note

Allow me to close with an image: Imagine walking into a workplace – it could be a bustling office, a factory floor, a classroom, a virtual team call – and seeing everyone engaged, unafraid, and valued. There's laughter, there's debate, there's resolve in tough moments, and learning in mistakes. People are not just executing tasks, they're growing, supporting each other, and finding purpose in their work. At the center of that environment is a leader – perhaps quietly in the background – who has cultivated this atmosphere. A leader who remembers what it felt like to be a child – curious, hopeful, at times insecure – and who channels that memory into guiding others with empathy and vision.

Be that leader. The one who brings out the best in people not by chance, but by care and design. The one who leads with both head and heart. The one who transforms workplaces into communities and tasks into avenues for fulfillment. The one who doesn't just achieve success, but significance – because they leave people better than they found them.

If you ever doubt the impact of such leadership, recall one more story: A seasoned CEO was retiring and in his farewell speech, he didn't list revenue growth or stock prices. Instead, he told a story of an employee who came up to him years after they'd worked together and said, "You changed my life. You believed in me when I didn't believe in myself. I've tried to do the same for others ever since." The CEO said that single comment meant more than any financial metric he'd hit. It was his legacy living on in another.

That is the power of being the leader you (and others) needed. It is legacy-building in the truest sense – a human legacy.

As you step forward from here, keep your inner child in sight as a friendly advisor – they'll remind you to stay humble, to stay playful, and to care deeply. Keep your vision clear, your heart healed and open, your trust strong, and your spirit resilient. In doing so, you not only become the leader you needed; you become the leader *needed in the world today.*

Lead on – with insight, with empathy, and with the knowledge that every great leader was once a child, and every child can grow up to be a great leader when someone lights the way. Your transformed leadership can be that light.

APPENDICES – THE LEADER WAS ONCE A CHILD

Appendix A: Self-Assessment & Reflection Toolkit

Attachment Style Self-Assessment

Answer each of the following with True or False:

1. I often worry others won't like or respect me unless I succeed.
2. I find it hard to trust others with important tasks.
3. I prefer to handle things alone, even when help is available.
4. I often need reassurance that I'm doing well.
5. I feel uncomfortable being emotionally open with others.

Scoring:

- Mostly True to 1 & 4: Anxious Attachment
- Mostly True to 2 & 5: Avoidant Attachment
- Mostly False: Secure Attachment

Inner Child Journaling Prompts

1. What did you most need as a child that you didn't receive consistently?
2. What were you often praised for?
3. What were you often criticized for?
4. Recall a moment you felt especially safe or unsafe — what was happening?

5. If your 8-year-old self could give your current leadership style advice, what would they say?

Leadership Behavior Mapping Worksheet

Step 1: Identify a recurring leadership behavior that frustrates you.

Step 2: Recall childhood situations with similar emotions or expectations.

Step 3: Write the belief learned in that moment (e.g., 'I must prove my worth.').

Step 4: Draft a reframed belief (e.g., 'My value isn't tied to perfection.').

APPENDIX B: RESEARCH FOUNDATIONS & FURTHER READING

Psychological Theories Referenced

- Attachment Theory: John Bowlby & Mary Ainsworth
- Emotional Intelligence: Daniel Goleman
- Schema Therapy: Jeffrey Young
- Vulnerability in Leadership: Brené Brown

Recommended Books & Articles

- 'The Body Keeps the Score' by Bessel van der Kolk
- 'Dare to Lead' by Brené Brown
- 'Primal Leadership' by Daniel Goleman
- 'Attached' by Amir Levine and Rachel Heller

REFERENCES

How your childhood affects your leadership skills - TrainingZone

https://trainingzone.co.uk/how-your-childhood-is-affecting-your-leadership-skills/

interviews- Summary.docx

file://file-Y9XqCrERTuH57rZpKjvcni

18 Schemas That Change the Way You See the World | Psychology Today

Leadership

https://www.psychologytoday.com/us/blog/the-savvy-psychologist/202201/18-schemas-that-change-the-way-you-see-the-world

Schema Theory: Why leaders do the dysfunctional things they do - WIRTSCHAFTSPSYCHOLOGIE HEUTE

https://www.wirtschaftspsychologie-heute.de/schema-theory-why-leaders-do-the-dysfunctional-things-they-do/

Attachment Styles at Work:

How the Past Shapes Leadership | Psychology Today

https://www.psychologytoday.com/us/blog/transforming-the-status-quo/202412/attachment-styles-at-work-how-the-past- shapes-leadership

Emotional Intelligence Frameworks, Charts, Diagrams & Graphs

https://positivepsychology.com/emotional-intelligence-frameworks/

mediatorsbeyondborders.org

https://mediatorsbeyondborders.org/wp-content/uploads/2020/01/managing-your-triggers-toolkit.pdf

CPTSD in the Workplace: Trigger Toolkit | by Cyndi Bennett | Medium

https://blog.cyndibennettconsulting.com/cptsd-in-the-workplace-trigger-toolkit-26e17dca76b7

AUTHOR BIO

Dr. Kartik Nagendraa brings nearly two decades of leadership experience across strategy, marketing, operations, and HR, with senior roles at global organisations including Wipro and Accenture. He is a trusted advisor to business leaders, universities, and global institutions. A bestselling author and thought leader, his work has appeared in Forbes, Economic Times, and Business World, and he has spoken at Wharton, Duke, UCLA, and other leading universities. He is a LinkedIn top voice, recognised among the top marketing consultants globally and endorsed by Marshall Goldsmith, he is also an ICF certified coach and serves on advisory panels for Harvard Business Review and Lean In India HeforShe initiative, helping leaders unlock their true potential.

Gauri Das is an engineer turned HR leader with dual master's degrees in Human Resources and Psychology, whose journey from a small village and vernacular education to the global leadership stage defines what is possible. Today, she is a two time TEDx speaker, award winning HR professional, certified coach, and SVP and Head of HR at a European bank subsidiary. Recognised by platforms such as Economic Times, LinkedIn, and global leadership forums, she is a LinkedIn Top Voice with over 70,000 followers. A passionate advocate for women's leadership, Gauri mentors and coaches professionals through initiatives like Lean In circles and WICCI, driven by her belief to be limitless and live as a possibilitarian.